SALADS

SALADS

Mmmm... salads, is there any other combination of foods that is so fresh and crisp, so bursting with color and seemingly with the power to make you feel as though you are getting healthier with each and every bite? Salads are a wonderful way to balance out a heavy dinner, or start or finish a light meal, and just as wonderful served on their own as the star attraction. Their versatility is unlimited — only your preferences and produce availability will set any restrictions. Preparing the perfect salad is quite simple but begins long before you start the recipe — a fact that is often forgotten. First, you must search out the freshest vegetables you can find, inspecting items carefully for hidden blemishes or just plain poor quality. Secondly, it is essential that all vegetables be thoroughly washed in plenty of cold water — tomatoes, cucumbers, everything! Thirdly, they must also be thoroughly dried (especially greens), otherwise the dressing you so carefully blended will not adhere properly, causing the whole salad to taste watery. And lastly, they should be trimmed, pared, cut as suggested in the recipe and assembled in a large serving bowl for tossing. Even if the salad is small it should be tossed with the dressing in a large bowl to make sure everything is evenly coated. Enjoy.

Summer Salad

(serves 4)

1 SERVING	571 CALORIES	20g CARBOHYDRATE
5g PROTEIN	55g FAT	2.8g FIBER

1 tbsp	(15 ml) strong mustard
1 tsp	(5 ml) chopped chives
1 tsp	(5 ml) chopped parsley
1 tbsp	(15 ml) green peppercorns, mashed
¼ cup	(50 ml) wine vinegar
1 cup	(250 ml) olive oil
1	head Romaine lettuce, leaves in bite-size pieces
1 cup	(250 ml) cooked green beans
1 cup	(250 ml) cooked yellow beans
1 cup	(250 ml) cooked green peas
2	carrots, pared and in fine julienne
	salt and pepper
	few drops lemon juice

Place mustard, chives, parsley, peppercorns, salt and lemon juice in bowl. Whisk in vinegar.

Incorporate oil in thin stream, whisking constantly. Correct seasoning.

Place remaining ingredients in large salad bowl. Pour on vinaigrette to taste, toss and serve.

Vegetable Salad with Cheese Dressing

(serves 4)

1 SERVING	403 CALORIES	36g CARBOHYDRATE
25g PROTEIN	22g FAT	2.1g FIBER

1	Boston lettuce
1	small Romaine lettuce
1	celery stalk, thinly sliced
2 cups	(500 ml) cooked cauliflower
3	canned beets, in julienne
½ cup	(125 ml) well-cooked bacon, chopped
1 cup	(250 ml) garlic croutons
3 oz	(90 g) blue cheese
4 tbsp	(60 ml) sour cream
3 tbsp	(45 ml) lemon juice
1 tbsp	(15 ml) cider vinegar
3 tbsp	(45 ml) heavy cream
	salt and pepper

Wash and dry both lettuces. Tear leaves into smaller pieces and place in large bowl.

Add celery, cauliflower, beets, bacon and croutons.

Mix blue cheese, sour cream and remaining ingredients in food processor until smooth.

Correct seasoning, pour dressing over salad and toss well. Serve.

Mixed Vegetable Side Salad

(serves 4)

1 SERVING	165 CALORIES	7g CARBOHYDRATE
7g PROTEIN	12g FAT	2.9g FIBER

1	English cucumber
1	head broccoli, in flowerets, cooked
1	carrot, pared and grated
3 oz	(90 g) cheddar cheese, in julienne
	salt and pepper
	vinaigrette of your choice

Do not peel cucumber. Cut in half lengthwise, remove seeds and slice.

Place cucumber in bowl with cooked broccoli, carrot and cheese. Season and toss.

Pour in vinaigrette, toss again and serve.

Eggplant Salad

(serves 4)

1 SERVING	637 CALORIES	48g CARBOHYDRATE
12g PROTEIN	48g FAT	1.0g FIBER

2	garlic cloves, smashed and chopped
¼ cup	(50 ml) wine vinegar
¾ cup	(175 ml) olive oil
1 tbsp	(15 ml) lemon juice
1	small eggplant
4	potatoes, cooked in jackets and still hot
4	large tomatoes, skinned, cut in half and sliced
2	bunches asparagus, tips cooked and cut in half
1 cup	(250 ml) cubed pineapple, drained
4 tbsp	(60 ml) toasted slivered almonds
	salt and pepper
	vegetable oil

Preheat ovent to 400°F (200°C).

Place garlic, vinegar, olive oil, lemon juice, salt and pepper in small bowl; whisk together and set aside.

Cut eggplant lengthwise into slices ½ in (1.2 cm) thick. Cut into long strips and dice. Place eggplant on cookie sheet and brush generously with vegetable oil.

Cook 15 minutes in oven, turning pieces over often.

Transfer eggplant to large salad bowl.

Peel hot potatoes, cut in half and slice; add to salad bowl.

Add tomatoes, asparagus, pineapple and almonds to bowl. Pour in vinaigrette to taste, toss well, season and serve.

Lettuce and Fruit Salad

(serves 4)

1 SERVING	447 CALORIES	12g CARBOHYDRATE
3g PROTEIN	45g FAT	1.4g FIBER

4 tbsp	(60 ml) wine vinegar
⅔ cup	(150 ml) olive oil
1 tsp	(5 ml) sugar
1 tbsp	(15 ml) lemon juice
2	endives, separated, leaves cut in ½
1	small bunch watercress
1	Boston lettuce, in leaves
1	yellow pepper, cut in thin strips
2 cups	(500 ml) ripe strawberries, hulled
	salt and pepper

Using whisk, mix vinegar with oil, sugar and lemon juice; season well and set dressing aside.

Place endives and watercress in salad bowl. Tear lettuce leaves into smaller pieces and add to bowl with yellow pepper and strawberries.

Whisk dressing and pour over salad. Toss and serve.

The Best Bean Salad

(serves 4-6)

1 SERVING	420 CALORIES	35g CARBOHYDRATE
19g PROTEIN	26g FAT	2.0g FIBER

1½ cups	(375 ml) white beans, soaked in cold water overnight
1	carrot, sliced
1	onion, chopped
1 tsp	(5 ml) celery seed
2	bay leaves
1 tsp	(5 ml) basil
1 tsp	(5 ml) chopped parsley
1 cup	(250 ml) cooked red kidney beans
1 cup	(250 ml) black-eyed peas (ready to serve)
1 tsp	(5 ml) vegetable oil
4	slices back bacon, ¼ in (0.65 cm) thick, diced
1	medium onion, chopped
1	garlic clove, smashed and chopped
1 tbsp	(15 ml) strong mustard
¼ cup	(50 ml) raspberry wine vinegar
½ cup	(125 ml) olive oil
	salt and pepper

Drain beans and place in large saucepan. Add carrot, 1 chopped onion, celery seed, bay leaves, basil and parsley.

Pour in enough water to cover by 2 in (5 cm). Partially cover and cook 1½ hours, skimming as necessary during cooking.

Drain beans and vegetables; transfer to salad bowl.

Add kidney beans and peas; toss and set aside.

Heat vegetable oil in small frying pan. Cook bacon, remaining onion and garlic 3 to 4 minutes over medium-high heat or until browned.

Stir this into salad mixture.

Mix mustard, vinegar and oil together in small bowl; season well and whisk. Pour over beans, toss and serve warm or slightly chilled.

Drain beans and place in large saucepan with carrot, 1 chopped onion and seasonings. Cover with water and cook 1½ hours partially covered; skim as necessary.

Cook bacon with remaining onion and garlic in hot oil, then add to salad bowl.

Add kidney beans and peas to drained white beans and vegetables; toss and set aside.

Pour dressing over beans, toss and serve warm or cold.

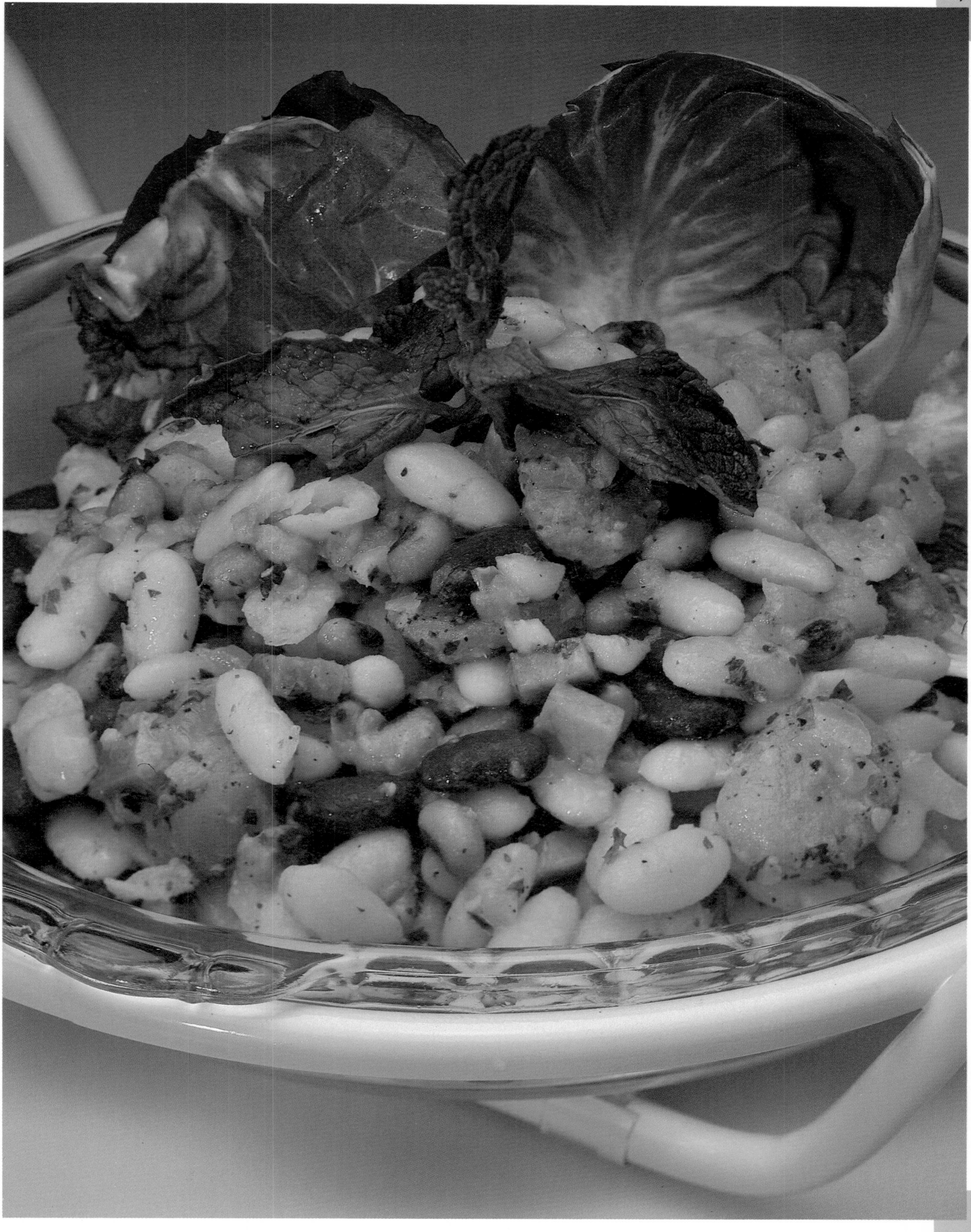

Tomato Mustard Salad

(serves 4)

1 SERVING	553 CALORIES	8g CARBOHYDRATE
5g PROTEIN	67g FAT	0.8g FIBER

4	ripe tomatoes, cut in ½ and sliced
2	shallots, finely chopped
1 tsp	(5 ml) chopped parsley
1 tsp	(5 ml) chopped chives
2	hard-boiled eggs, sliced
1 tbsp	(15 ml) Dijon mustard
¼ cup	(50 ml) wine vinegar
1 cup	(250 ml) olive oil
	salt and pepper

Place tomatoes, shallots, parsley, chives and eggs in bowl; season well.

Place mustard, vinegar and oil in another bowl. Mix together with whisk and season well.

Pour vinaigrette over tomatoes to taste, toss and serve.

Light Side Salad

(serves 4)

1 SERVING	184 CALORIES	28g CARBOHYDRATE
4g PROTEIN	8g FAT	1.4g FIBER

3	bananas, peeled and sliced
2	celery stalks, thinly sliced
12	cherry tomatoes, halved
1 tbsp	(15 ml) lemon juice
4 tbsp	(60 ml) sour cream
¼ cup	(50 ml) chopped walnuts
	salt and pepper
	Boston lettuce leaves

Place bananas, celery and tomatoes in bowl. Mix in lemon juice and sour cream; season well.

Arrange lettuce leaves on side plates, add salad and sprinkle servings with chopped walnuts.

Cucumber Salad with Sour Cream Dressing

(serves 4)

1 SERVING	79 CALORIES	12g CARBOHYDRATE
3g PROTEIN	3g FAT	1.1g FIBER

1	cucumber, peeled, seeded and sliced
2	celery stalks, sliced
12	cherry tomatoes, halved
3	hearts of palm, sliced
1 tbsp	(15 ml) chopped parsley
4 tbsp	(40 ml) sour cream
¼ tsp	(1 ml) dry mustard
1 tsp	(5 ml) red wine vinegar
	juice 1 lemon
	pinch sugar
	salt and pepper
	alfalfa sprouts for decoration
	pinch paprika

Place cucumber, celery, tomatoes, hearts of palm and parsley in salad bowl. Toss gently.

Mix together remaining ingredients with the exception of alfalfa sprouts and paprika.

Pour dressing over salad and toss to coat evenly. Arrange servings on small bed of alfalfa sprouts and sprinkle with a dash of paprika.

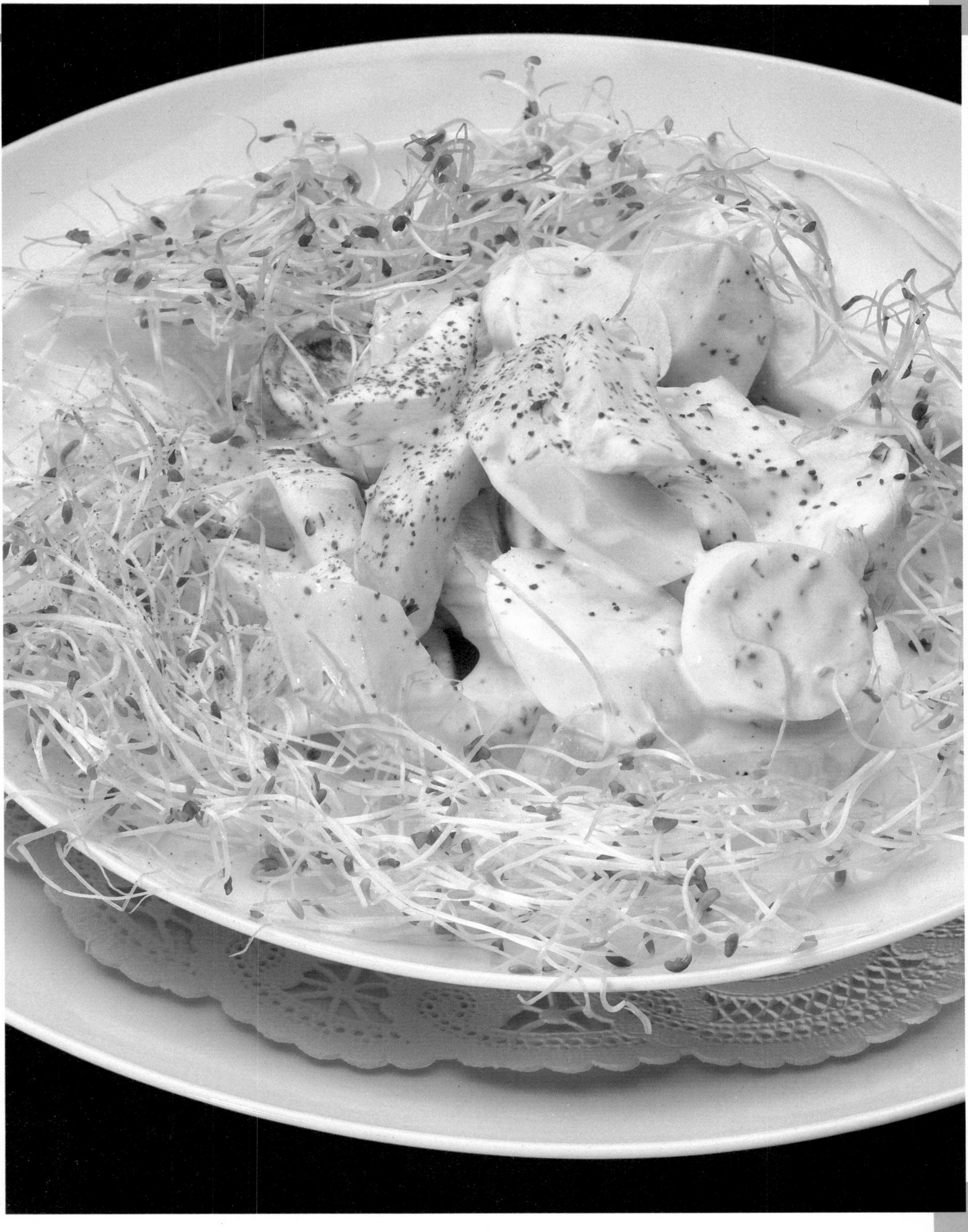

Watercress Salad

(serves 4)

1 SERVING	614 CALORIES	12g CARBOHYDRATE
18g PROTEIN	57g FAT	1.7g FIBER

¼ cup	(50 ml) wine vinegar
½ cup	(125 ml) olive oil
½	zucchini, in julienne and blanched
¼ lb	(125 g) green beans, pared and cooked
2	endives, leaves separated
1	small bunch watercress
6 oz	(170 g) cheddar cheese, in julienne
2	hard-boiled eggs, sliced
½ cup	(125 ml) chopped walnuts
½	ripe avocado, sliced thick
	salt and pepper
	juice 1 lemon

Mix vinegar, salt, pepper and lemon juice together in small bowl. Very slowly incorporate oil while mixing constantly with whisk. Set dressing aside.

Arrange remaining ingredients in large salad bowl. Pour in dressing, toss and serve.

Endive Salad Robert

(serves 4)

1 SERVING	429 CALORIES	33g CARBOHYDRATE
22g PROTEIN	21g FAT	2.7g FIBER

6	artichoke bottoms, cut in 3
5	endives, leaves well washed
1	cooked chicken breast, skinned and in julienne
1	Boston lettuce
2	tomatoes, cored and in wedges
½	cucumber, peeled, seeded and sliced
1	onion, finely chopped
¼ cup	(50 ml) wine vinegar
1 cup	(250 ml) dry white wine
⅔ cup	(150 ml) brown sauce, heated
	salt and pepper
	your favorite vinaigrette

Place artichoke bottoms, endives and chicken in salad bowl.

Tear washed lettuce leaves into smaller pieces; add to bowl along with tomatoes and cucumber.

Place onion in small saucepan. Add vinegar and wine and season with pepper. Cook 4 minutes over medium-high heat.

Mix in brown sauce and season; continue cooking 2 minutes.

Mix this sauce to taste with your favorite vinaigrette, then pour over salad, toss and serve.

Refrigerate remaining brown sauce for other uses.

Endives with Cucumber Mayonnaise

(serves 4)

1 SERVING	576 CALORIES	24g CARBOHYDRATE
42g PROTEIN	35g FAT	0.7g FIBER

½	cucumber, peeled and seeded
1¼ cups	(300 ml) mayonnaise
¼ tsp	(1 ml) paprika
¼ tsp	(1 ml) Tabasco sauce
1 tsp	(5 ml) lemon juice
3	endives, separated, leaves cut in ½
1	apple, peeled, cored and sliced
4	slices Black Forest ham, in julienne
2 tbsp	(30 ml) pine nuts
	salt and pepper

Place cucumber in food processor and purée.

Add mayonnaise, paprika, Tabasco sauce, lemon juice, salt and pepper; blend 30 seconds. Set aside.

Arrange endives, apple and ham in large salad bowl. Add cucumber mayonnaise to taste, mix well and serve.

Garnish individual portions with pine nuts.

Potato Bacon Salad

(serves 4)

1 SERVING	263 CALORIES	31g CARBOHYDRATE
10g PROTEIN	22g FAT	0.8g FIBER

2	green onions, chopped
1	shallot, chopped
6	potatoes, cooked in jackets and still hot, peeled and cubed
1 tbsp	(15 ml) chopped parsley
4	slices crisp bacon, chopped
3 tbsp	(45 ml) wine vinegar
⅓ cup	(75 ml) olive oil
3 tbsp	(45 ml) dry white wine
	salt and pepper

Place onions, shallot, potatoes and parsley in large bowl; toss and season.

Add bacon and remaining ingredients; toss gently but well.

Cool before serving.

Warm Potato Salad

(serves 4)

1 SERVING	236 CALORIES	18g CARBOHYDRATE
5g PROTEIN	16g FAT	0.5g FIBER

4	medium potatoes
2	hard-boiled eggs, chopped
2 tbsp	(30 ml) wine vinegar
4 tbsp	(60 ml) olive oil
1 tbsp	(15 ml) chopped chives
	salt and pepper
	few sprigs fresh watercress

Cook potatoes in jackets in salted boiling water.

When cooked, drain well and let stand 5 minutes in saucepan.

Peel potatoes, cut in ½ and slice; place in bowl.

Add eggs and toss gently. Add remaining ingredients, except watercress, and toss well.

Serve salad decorated with watercress.

Potato Salad with Mussels

(serves 4)

1 SERVING	470 CALORIES	27g CARBOHYDRATE
20g PROTEIN	32g FAT	1.3g FIBER

1 tsp	(5 ml) curry powder
1 tsp	(5 ml) sugar
4 tbsp	(60 ml) wine vinegar
½ cup	(125 ml) olive oil
½ tsp	(2 ml) lemon juice
1 tbsp	(15 ml) chopped parsley
1	garlic clove, smashed and chopped
1	bunch asparagus tips, cooked
4	potatoes, cooked in jackets and still hot
2	hard-boiled eggs, quartered
1½ cups	(375 ml) marinated mussels, drained
2 tbsp	(30 ml) chopped sweet pimento
	few blanched snow pea pods
	salt and pepper

Mix curry, sugar, wine vinegar, oil, salt and pepper together in bowl. Whisk until completely incorporated.

Blend in lemon juice, parsley and garlic; set dressing aside.

Place cooked asparagus in large salad bowl.

Peel hot potatoes and cut into large cubes. Add to bowl along with remaining ingredients.

Whisk dressing again and pour over salad. Toss and serve.

Hot Veggie Side Salad

(serves 4)

1 SERVING	187 CALORIES	14g CARBOHYDRATE
3g PROTEIN	10g FAT	1.5g FIBER

½	red pepper, diced large
½	yellow pepper, diced large
1	onion, diced large
1 cup	(250 ml) dry white wine
1	celery stalk, sliced thick
3	green onions, in 2.5 cm (1 in) lengths
¼	head broccoli, in flowerets
⅓	cucumber, peeled, halved, seeded and sliced thick
⅓	zucchini, sliced thick
¼	Chinese cabbage, sliced thick
2	garlic cloves, smashed and chopped
1 tbsp	(15 ml) chopped parsley
2	bay leaves
1 tsp	(5 ml) basil
3 tbsp	(45 ml) olive oil
3 tbsp	(45 ml) wine vinegar
	salt and pepper
	fresh mint to taste
	fresh dill to taste
	juice ½ lime

Place peppers, diced onion, wine, celery and green onions in skillet. Season, cover and cook 3 minutes over high heat.

Add all remaining ingredients, except lime juice, and cook 6 minutes covered over medium-high heat.

Sprinkle in lime juice and serve immediately.

1 Cut and trim the vegetables as neatly as possible to further enhance the finished product.

2 Place peppers, diced onion, wine, celery and green onions in skillet. Season, cover and cook 3 minutes over high heat.

3 Add all remaining ingredients, except lime juice, and cook 6 minutes covered over medium-high heat.

4 Sprinkle in lime juice and serve immediately.

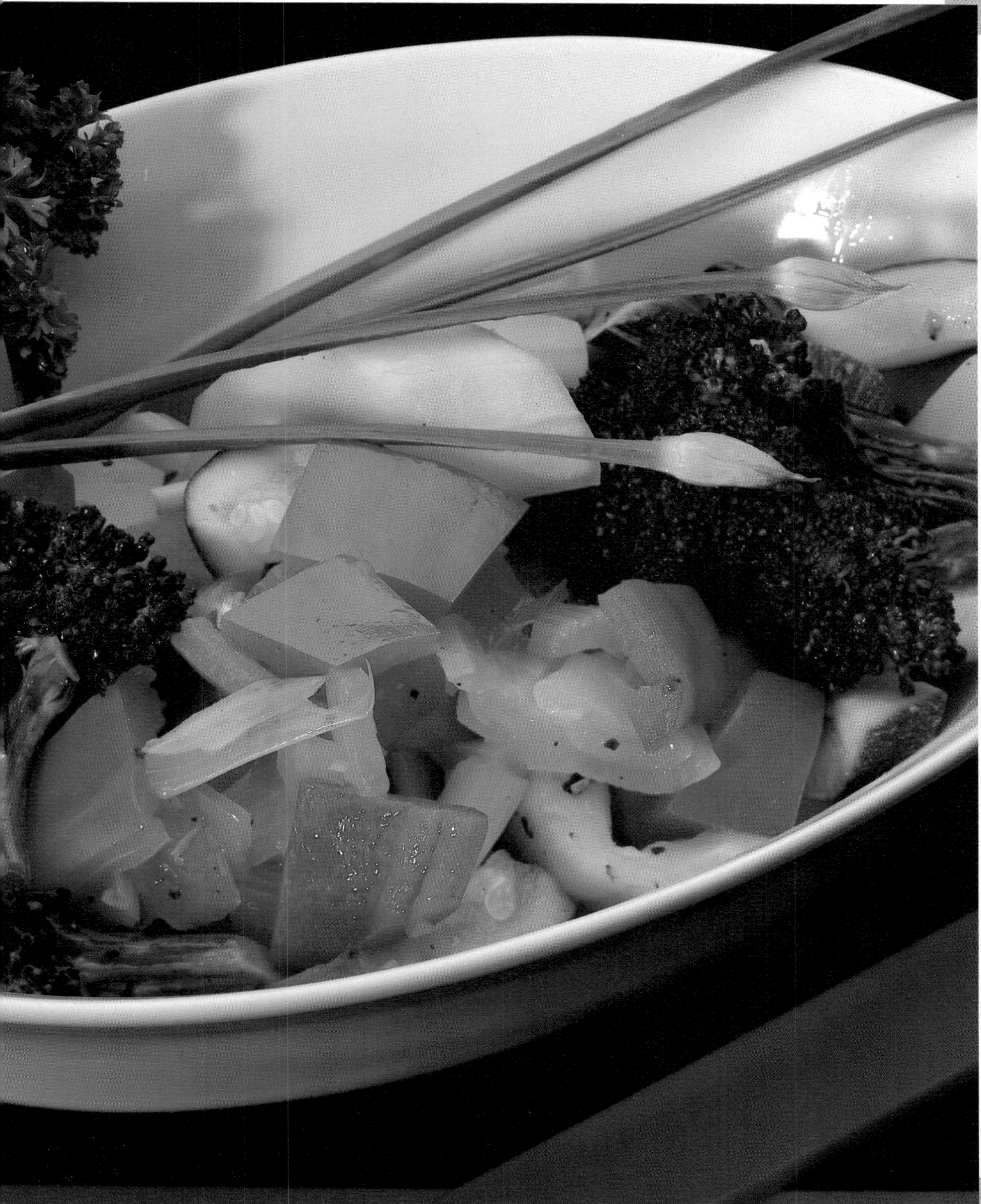

Marinated Mushrooms

(serves 4)

1 SERVING	335 CALORIES	14g CARBOHYDRATE
6g PROTEIN	31g FAT	1.8g FIBER

2 lb	(900 g) fresh mushrooms, well cleaned
1 tbsp	(15 ml) butter
1 tbsp	(15 ml) chopped parsley
1	lemon, cut in ½
1 cup	(250 ml) dry red wine
¼ cup	(50 ml) wine vinegar
½ cup	(125 ml) olive oil
1 tsp	(5 ml) tarragon
¼ tsp	(1 ml) ground cloves
1	shallot, chopped
	salt and pepper

Place mushrooms, butter and parsley in saucepan. Squeeze juice from lemon halves, add to saucepan and season well.

Pour in wine, vinegar and olive oil. Mix well.

Add remaining ingredients, season and cook 8 to 10 minutes over high heat with cover. Stir once or twice during cooking.

Cool mushrooms before serving.

Arrange on fresh lettuce leaves with slices of lemon if desired.

Place mushrooms, butter and parsley in saucepan. Squeeze juice from lemon halves, add to saucepan and season well.

Pour in vinegar.

Pour in wine.

Pour in olive oil.

Rice Salad with Lemon Dressing

(serves 4)

1 SERVING	622 CALORIES	33g CARBOHYDRATE
27g PROTEIN	43g FAT	1.3g FIBER

4 tbsp	(60 ml) lemon juice
1	egg yolk
¾ cup	(175 ml) sunflower oil
2 cups	(500 ml) cooked rice
1	red pepper, diced small
1	celery stalk, sliced
16	cooked shrimp, cut in 3
1	bunch asparagus, tips cooked and cut in 1 in (2.5 cm) lengths
¼ lb	(125 g) cooked green beans, cut in 2
1 tbsp	(15 ml) chopped parsley
	pinch sugar
	dash paprika
	salt and pepper

Place lemon juice, egg yolk, sugar, paprika, salt and pepper in small bowl. Whisk together until well incorporated.

Incorporate oil in thin stream while whisking constantly. Season very well.

Place remaining ingredients in large salad bowl. Pour in dressing, season and toss well. Serve.

Chick Pea Salad

(serves 4)

1 SERVING	521 CALORIES	50g CARBOHYDRATE
17g PROTEIN	6g FAT	3.3g FIBER

19 oz	(540 ml) can chick peas, drained
¼ lb	(250 g) cooked green beans
1½ cups	(375 ml) marinated cauliflower, drained
1 tbsp	(15 ml) chopped parsley
1	yellow pepper, diced
1 tbsp	(15 ml) tarragon
¼ cup	(50 ml) cider vinegar
½ tsp	(2 ml) sugar
½ cup	(125 ml) olive oil
1 tsp	(5 ml) fresh chopped mint
	salt and pepper
	few drops lemon juice
	Tabasco sauce to taste

Place chick peas, beans, cauliflower, parsley and yellow pepper in large salad bowl.

In separate bowl, mix together remaining ingredients, whisking until well incorporated.

Pour dressing over salad, toss and serve.

Hearty Pasta Salad

(serves 4)

1 SERVING	395 CALORIES	40g CARBOHYDRATE
13g PROTEIN	21g FAT	1.9g FIBER

1	garlic clove, smashed and chopped
1 tbsp	(15 ml) Dijon mustard
1	egg yolk
1	hard-boiled egg
¼ tsp	(1 ml) paprika
⅓ cup	(75 ml) olive oil
1½ cups	(375 ml) cooked medium pasta bows
1 cup	(250 ml) cooked red kidney beans
½ cup	(125 ml) cooked green peas
½ cup	(125 ml) blanched diced carrots
1	green onion, chopped
2	artichoke bottoms, sliced
1	celery stalk, sliced
1	leaf Chinese lettuce, sliced
	salt and pepper
	grated Parmesan cheese to taste
	juice 1 lemon

Place garlic, mustard and egg yolk in small bowl; whisk together.

Add hard-boiled egg by forcing through sieve. Whisk in paprika, salt, pepper, dash of Parmesan cheese and lemon juice.

Incorporate oil in thin stream while whisking constantly. Set dressing aside.

Place remaining ingredients in large salad bowl and pour in dressing. Toss, correct seasoning and serve.

Add hard-boiled egg to dressing ingredients by forcing through sieve.

Whisk in paprika, salt, pepper, dash of Parmesan cheese and lemon juice.

Incorporate oil in thin stream while whisking constantly.

Pour dressing over salad ingredients, toss, correct seasoning and serve.

Chicken Salad

(serves 4)

1 SERVING	286 CALORIES	18g CARBOHYDRATE
32g PROTEIN	10g FAT	1.0g FIBER

2	chicken breasts, skinned and halved
1	celery stalk, sliced thick on angle
1	parsley sprig
4	lemon slices
1	onion, diced large
¼ tsp	(1 ml) celery seed
1	green onion, chopped
1	celery stalk, sliced
2	hard-boiled eggs, sliced
¼ tsp	(1 ml) paprika
6	water chestnuts, sliced
½ cup	(125 ml) seedless green grapes
2 tbsp	(30 ml) diced pimento
3 tbsp	(45 ml) mayonnaise
1 tsp	(5 ml) curry powder
	salt and pepper
	several cherry tomatoes, halved
	juice 1 lemon

Place chicken, first celery stalk, parsley sprig, lemon slices, diced onion, celery seed, salt and pepper in saucepan. Pour in enough water to cover. Cover and cook about 18 minutes over medium heat, depending on size of breasts.

When chicken is cooked, drain and discard other ingredients. Bone chicken and cut meat in large slices.

Place green onion, other celery stalk, eggs and paprika in bowl. Add chicken and season well.

Mix in water chestnuts, grapes, pimento and tomatoes; toss slightly.

Mix in remaining ingredients until well incorporated and serve salad on lettuce leaves.

1 Place chicken, first celery stalk, parsley sprig, lemon slices, diced onion, celery seed, salt and pepper in saucepan. Add water to cover and cook, covered, about 18 minutes over medium heat depending on size of breasts.

3 Add cooked chicken and season.

2 Place green onion, other celery stalk, eggs and paprika in bowl.

4 Add remaining ingredients, mix until well incorporated and correct seasoning.

Chicken and Beef Salad

(serves 4)

1 SERVING	621 CALORIES	7g CARBOHYDRATE
38g PROTEIN	49g FAT	0.9g FIBER

1 tbsp	(15 ml) Dijon mustard
1 tsp	(5 ml) chopped fresh tarragon
1	garlic clove, smashed and chopped
3 tbsp	(45 ml) wine vinegar
2 tbsp	(30 ml) lemon juice
¾ cup	(175 ml) olive oil
1	head Chinese lettuce
1	cooked chicken breast, skinned and boned
1 cup	(250 ml) leftover cooked steak, in strips
2	tomatoes, cut in half, then in wedges
1	celery stalk, sliced
2	hard-boiled eggs, sliced
	salt and pepper

Place mustard, tarragon, garlic, vinegar and lemon juice in small bowl; whisk together.

Incorporate oil in thin stream while whisking constantly. Correct seasoning and set aside.

Wash and dry lettuce; tear leaves into smaller pieces. Cut cooked chicken breast into strips; place in salad bowl with lettuce.

Add steak, tomatoes, celery and eggs to salad bowl. Toss everything well.

Whisk vinaigrette and pour over salad to taste. Toss well, season and serve.

Chinatown Salad

(serves 4)

1 SERVING	263 CALORIES	27g CARBOHYDRATE
19g PROTEIN	2g FAT	1.9g FIBER

1	cooked chicken breast, skinned, boned and sliced thick
1 tbsp	(15 ml) chopped fresh ginger
2	garlic cloves, smashed and chopped
1 tbsp	(15 ml) soya sauce
1½ cups	(375 ml) shredded radicchio
1 cup	(250 ml) cooked green peas
1 cup	(250 ml) bean sprouts
1	yellow pepper, thinly sliced
2	green onions, chopped
3 tbsp	(45 ml) red wine vinegar
¼ cup	(50 ml) sesame oil
	salt and pepper

Place chicken, ginger, garlic, soya sauce, radicchio and green peas in bowl. Season well.

Add bean sprouts, yellow pepper and green onions. Pour in wine vinegar and oil. Toss everything to incorporate well, correct seasoning and serve.

Place chicken,
ginger, garlic and
soya sauce in bowl.

Add radicchio
and green peas;
season well.

Add bean
sprouts, yellow
pepper and green
onions. Pour in wine
vinegar.

Pour in oil, toss
and correct
seasoning.

Elegant Strawberry and Shrimp Salad

(serves 4)

1 SERVING	459 CALORIES	70g CARBOHYDRATE
31g PROTEIN	6g FAT	1.8g FIBER

¾ lb	(375 g) cooked shrimp
12	canned baby corn on the cob
1	pear, peeled and sliced
½ lb	(250 g) ripe strawberries, hulled and halved
4 tbsp	(60 ml) sour cream
1 tsp	(5 ml) dry mustard
1 tbsp	(15 ml) apple cider
1 tsp	(5 ml) ground ginger
	juice 1 lemon
	pinch sugar
	few drops Tabasco sauce

Place shrimp, corn, pear and strawberries in salad bowl.

Mix sour cream with mustard; add lemon juice.

Whisk in cider, sugar, ginger and Tabasco sauce.

Pour over salad and mix well. Serve on lettuce leaves if desired.

Shrimp and Pepper Salad

(serves 4)

1 SERVING	412 CALORIES	9g CARBOHYDRATE
17g PROTEIN	35g FAT	1.5g FIBER

2 tbsp	(30 ml) vegetable oil
1	onion, thinly sliced
2	yellow peppers, thinly sliced
2	garlic cloves, smashed and chopped
1½ cups	(375 ml) thinly sliced eggplant
½ lb	(250 g) cooked shrimp
3 tbsp	(45 ml) wine vinegar
½ cup	(125 ml) olive oil
	salt and pepper

Heat vegetable oil in large frying pan. Cook onion, peppers, garlic and eggplant 7 minutes over medium heat with cover. Stir 2 to 3 times during cooking and season well.

Remove vegetables from pan and transfer to salad bowl; set aside.

Add shrimp, vinegar and olive oil to frying pan; season well. Cook 1 to 2 minutes over medium-high heat.

Drain most of the oil off, then add shrimp to salad bowl. Toss and cool slightly before serving.

Scallop Salad

(serves 4)

1 SERVING	309 CALORIES	28g CARBOHYDRATE
35g PROTEIN	6g FAT	1.6g FIBER

3	large potatoes, peeled and cut into balls
1 lb	(500 g) large mushrooms, quartered
1 tbsp	(15 ml) lemon juice
1 tbsp	(15 ml) oil
¼ tsp	(1 ml) fennel seed
1 lb	(500 g) scallops
1 tbsp	(15 ml) chopped parsley
3 tbsp	(45 ml) sour cream
1 tbsp	(15 ml) Dijon mustard
1 tbsp	(15 ml) chopped pimento
	juice 1 lemon
	salt and pepper

Place potato balls in saucepan, season with salt and pour in enough cold water to cover. Bring to boil. Continue cooking 5 minutes over medium heat.

Add mushrooms, 1 tbsp (15 ml) lemon juice, oil and fennel seed; continue cooking 2 minutes.

Drop in scallops and finish cooking 1 minute.

Drain well and transfer boiled ingredients to salad bowl; sprinkle with parsley.

Squeeze in juice of 1 lemon and season well. Mix in sour cream, mustard and pimento; toss until all is evenly coated.

Serve.

Fish and Vegetable Salad

(serves 4)

1 SERVING	431 CALORIES	18g CARBOHYDRATE
15g PROTEIN	35g FAT	2.1g FIBER

3 tbsp	(45 ml) wine vinegar
2	garlic cloves, smashed and chopped
1 tbsp	(15 ml) soya sauce
½ tsp	(2 ml) sugar
½ cup	(125 ml) olive oil
2 tbsp	(30 ml) vegetable oil
2	sole filets, cut in 2.5 cm (1 in) pieces
2 cups	(500 ml) broccoli flowerets, blanched
¼ lb	(125 g) snow peas, blanched
6	cooked asparagus, cut in 2.5 cm (1 in) lengths
6	cherry tomatoes, halved
2 tbsp	(30 ml) chopped fresh chives
6	water chestnuts, sliced
¼ tsp	(1 ml) ground ginger
½ tsp	(2 ml) ground cumin
	juice 1 lemon
	salt and pepper

Whisk vinegar, garlic, soya, sugar, olive oil and lemon juice together until well incorporated; set aside.

Heat remaining oil in large frying pan. Cook fish 2 minutes each side over high heat.

Add broccoli and pea pods; mix well.

Add remaining ingredients, season to taste and cook 3 to 4 minutes over high heat.

Transfer mixture to large salad bowl. Whisk dressing and pour over ingredients; toss well and serve immediately.

Cook fish in hot oil for 2 minutes on each side over high heat.

Add broccoli and pea pods; mix well.

Add remaining ingredients, season to taste and cook 3 to 4 minutes over high heat.

Pour prepared dressing over salad, toss and serve.

Penne with Crab

(serves 4)

1 SERVING	494 CALORIES	40g CARBOHYDRATE
14g PROTEIN	30g FAT	0.6g FIBER

¼ cup	(50 ml) wine vinegar
1 tbsp	(15 ml) chopped parsley
½ cup	(125 ml) olive oil
1 tbsp	(15 ml) Dijon mustard
1 tsp	(5 ml) sugar
1 tsp	(5 ml) tarragon
¼ cup	(50 ml) grated Parmesan cheese
1	shallot, finely chopped
2	garlic cloves, smashed and chopped
¼ tsp	(1 ml) Tabasco sauce
3 cups	(750 ml) cooked penne
5	cooked asparagus, diced
2	hearts of palm, sliced
4.25 oz	(120 g) can crabmeat, well drained
2 tbsp	(30 ml) chopped pickled sweet pimento
	salt and pepper
	lettuce leaves for serving

Whisk together vinegar, parsley and oil until well incorporated.

Add mustard, sugar, tarragon, cheese, shallot, garlic, Tabasco, salt and pepper; continue whisking until vinaigrette has thickened.

Place remaining ingredients in salad bowl. Pour in vinaigrette, season and toss. Serve on lettuce leaves.

Whisk together vinegar, parsley and oil until well incorporated.

Add mustard, sugar, tarragon, cheese, shallot, garlic, Tabasco, salt and pepper; continue whisking until thickened.

Place salad ingredients in bowl.

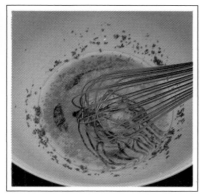

Pour in vinaigrette, season and toss.

Fancy Meal Salad

(serves 4)

1 SERVING	306 CALORIES	41g CARBOHYDRATE
13g PROTEIN	13g FAT	4.2g FIBER

3	pears, peeled and cut in wedges
½ lb	(250 g) white mushrooms, in julienne
3 cups	(500 ml) cooked green beans
1	yellow pepper, thinly sliced
1 cup	(250 ml) seedless green grapes
5 oz	(142 g) can crabmeat, drained
1 tbsp	(15 ml) curry powder
3 tbsp	(45 ml) lemon juice
1 tbsp	(15 ml) horseradish
1 cup	(250 ml) sour cream
1 tbsp	(15 ml) chopped chives
	salt and pepper

Place pears, mushrooms, beans, yellow pepper, grapes and crabmeat in salad bowl.

Place curry powder, lemon juice and horseradish in small bowl; whisk together very well and season generously.

Add sour cream and chives; whisk again until incorporated. Season again to taste and pour over salad; toss and serve.

Herring Salad

(serves 4)

1 SERVING	595 CALORIES	29g CARBOHYDRATE
13g PROTEIN	49g FAT	1.0g FIBER

1	hard-boiled egg
1 tbsp	(15 ml) Dijon mustard
4 tbsp	(60 ml) wine vinegar
¾ cup	(175 ml) olive oil
1 tbsp	(15 ml) lemon juice
3	cooked marinated herring filets, cubed
3	apples, peeled, cored and sliced
3	cooked potatoes, peeled and sliced
2	pickles, in julienne
3	canned beets, sliced
	salt and pepper

Cut hard-boiled egg in half and force yolk and white through sieve into bowl.

Add mustard and vinegar; whisk well.

Incorporate oil in thin stream while whisking constantly. Mix in lemon juice and correct seasoning.

Place herring, apples, potatoes, pickles and beets in large salad bowl.

Pour in vinaigrette to taste, toss well and correct seasoning.

APPETIZERS

APPETIZERS

Appetizers, in their countless shapes and sizes, come to our tables in hopes of awakening sleepy palates by tantalizing our senses with a sampling of flavors and textures that are married to perfection. Whether served hot or cold, appetizers are meant to be eaten for the pure pleasure of eating, so should never be too filling or so complicated that they prevent the diner from enjoying the fleeting moments with ease. From the simplest open-faced canapé to servings of fancy Lobster Liza, appetizers encourage spontaneity not just with ingredients but with the way in which they are presented. If you are serving an assortment of buffet-style appetizers, try arranging the platters on different levels surrounded by attractive plates, cutlery and napkins. Although hot appetizers require a little more care and planning (so they can be served promptly), take a few extra minutes to decorate portions with fresh herbs or condiments such as pickles and olives. The recipes following offer you an interesting selection of hot and cold dishes to choose from. Remember that an appetizer doesn't necessarily have to reflect what the main meal is about — so make your choice by what strikes your fancy and have fun with it!

Lobster Liza

(serves 4-6)

1 SERVING	326 CALORIES	27g CARBOHYDRATE
25g PROTEIN	11g FAT	0.9g FIBER

2 tbsp	(30 ml) butter
2	shallots, chopped
1	green pepper, chopped
1 lb	(500 g) chopped lobster meat, cooked
1¼ cups	(300 ml) thick tomato sauce, heated
1 tbsp	(15 ml) lemon juice
½ cup	(125 ml) grated Parmesan cheese
	salt and pepper
	toasted white bread

Heat butter in sauce pan. Cook shallots and green pepper 3 minutes over low heat.

Mix in lobster meat and tomato sauce; season well and add lemon juice. Cook over low heat 2 to 3 minutes.

Correct seasoning and spoon mixture over toast. Top with cheese and broil 2 to 3 minutes in oven.

Deep-Fried Fish

(serves 4-6)

1 SERVING	460 CALORIES	53g CARBOHYDRATE
29g PROTEIN	14g FAT	trace FIBER

2 cups	(500 ml) crushed soda crackers
1	garlic clove, smashed and chopped
1 tbsp	(15 ml) curry powder
1 tbsp	(15 ml) celery seed
4	large sole filets
1½ cups	(375 ml) seasoned flour
3	beaten eggs
	pepper
	peanut oil

Mix crackers with garlic, curry powder and celery seed; set aside in bowl.

Cut fish into strips ½ in (1.2 cm) wide. Throughly coat in flour.

Dip fish strips in beaten eggs, then in soda cracker crumbs. Season well with pepper.

Deep-fry in hot oil for 2 minutes.

Pat dry with paper towels and serve with lemon wedges.

Hot Shrimp Kebabs

(serves 4)

1 SERVING	422 CALORIES	20g CARBOHYDRATE
32g PROTEIN	24g FAT	0.7g FIBER

24	shrimp, peeled and deveined
3 tbsp	(45 ml) sesame oil
1 tbsp	(15 ml) lemon juice
¼ tsp	(1 ml) Tabasco sauce
24	large cubes fresh pineapple
24	wedges red apple
	salt and pepper
	melted butter seasoned with lemon juice

Place shrimp, oil, lemon juice and Tabasco sauce in bowl. Marinate 30 minutes.

Alternate shrimp, pineapple and apple on short wooden skewers. Baste with melted lemon butter and season very well.

Place skewers on ovenproof platter and broil 3 minutes each side in oven. Baste frequently.

Smoked Salmon Canapés

(serves 4-6)

1 SERVING	658 CALORIES	47g CARBOHYDRATE
34g PROTEIN	36g FAT	-- FIBER

1 lb	(500 g) sliced smoked salmon
½ cup	(125 ml) soft butter
1 tbsp	(15 ml) lemon juice
¼ tsp	(1 ml) Tabasco sauce
1	loaf French bread, sliced
3 tbsp	(45 ml) capers
	pepper
	sliced hard-boiled eggs

Place 4 slices of salmon in food processor. Add butter, lemon juice, Tabasco sauce and pepper; blend 30 seconds.

Butter bread with mixture and top with remaining smoked salmon. Sprinkle canapés with capers and decorate platter with sliced boiled eggs.

Rice Canapés

(serves 6-8)

1 SERVING	336 CALORIES	49g CARBOHYDRATE
12g PROTEIN	10g FAT	trace FIBER

5	hard-boiled eggs, chopped
1 cup	(250 ml) cooked saffron rice
½	celery stalk, diced small
2	green onions, finely chopped
1 tsp	(5 ml) chopped chives
3 tbsp	(45 ml) mayonnaise
2 tbsp	(30 ml) sour cream
1 tsp	(5 ml) Worcestershire sauce
	juice ½ lemon
	salt and pepper
	sliced Italian bread

Place eggs, rice, celery, onions and chives in bowl; mix well.

Add mayonnaise, sour cream, Worcestershire sauce, lemon juice, salt and pepper; mix again until incorporated.

Spread over sliced Italian bread and serve.

Party Canapés

(serves 6)

1 SERVING	289 CALORIES	39g CARBOHYDRATE
7g PROTEIN	10g FAT	1.0g FIBER

4	stems watercress, finely chopped
1	celery stalk, chopped
1	red apple, peeled, cored, quartered and chopped
1 tbsp	(15 ml) pine nuts
1 tbsp	(15 ml) chopped parsley
1 tsp	(5 ml) curry powder
2 tbsp	(30 ml) mayonnaise
1 tbsp	(15 ml) sour cream
1 tsp	(5 ml) lemon juice
10-12	slices "party" light rye bread with caraway seeds
	salt and pepper
	halved cherry tomatoes for garnish

Mix all ingredients together except bread and tomatoes.

Season to taste, spread mixture over bread slices and garnish with halved cherry tomatoes. If desired serve with blanched broccoli.

Cold Beef Appetizer

(serves 4)

1 SERVING	866 CALORIES	60g CARBOHYDRATE
31g PROTEIN	56g FAT	0.5g FIBER

½ lb	(250 g) soft butter
1	medium onion, finely chopped
1	garlic clove, smashed and chopped
1 tbsp	(15 ml) paprika
1	loaf French bread
½ lb	(250 g) thin slices cooked roast beef
	few drops lemon juice
	salt and pepper

Heat 1 tbsp (15 ml) butter in small saucepan. Cook onion and garlic 3 minutes over medium heat.

Mix in paprika and continue cooking 1 minute. Remove and puree in food processor; set aside to cool.

Mix onion mixture, remaining butter, lemon juice, salt and pepper together until well incorporated.

Slice bread and toast in oven. Spread butter over pieces of bread and top with roast beef.

Serve cold with pickles.

Fancy Pastrami Canapés

(serves 4)

1 SERVING	569 CALORIES	17g CARBOHYDRATE
31g PROTEIN	41g FAT	trace FIBER

10	thin slices deli bread
4 tbsp	(60 ml) butter
1 tbsp	(15 ml) mustard
1 tsp	(5 ml) horseradish
10	slices pastrami
1 cup	(250 ml) fine herb pâté
2 tbsp	(30 ml) sour cream
	shredded lettuce for garnish

Place slices of bread on cutting board.

Mix butter with mustard and horseradish; spread evenly over bread.

Place slice of pastrami on each slice of bread, trim crusts and cut into two triangles.

Arrange canapés on shredded lettuce.

Mix pâté with sour cream until well blended. Place in pastry bag and decorate canapés with mixture.

Cheesy Crab Bread

(serves 6)

1 SERVING	335 CALORIES	26g CARBOHYDRATE
13g PROTEIN	20g FAT	trace FIBER

3 tbsp	(45 ml) butter
1	onion, chopped
¼ lb	(125 g) mushrooms, chopped
5 oz	(142 g) can crabmeat, drained
1¼ cups	(300 ml) white sauce, heated
8-10	slices white bread, toasted
½ cup	(125 ml) grated Emmenthal cheese
	salt and pepper
	few drops Tabasco sauce

Heat butter in saucepan. Cook onion and mushrooms 2 to 3 minutes over medium-high heat; season well and add Tabasco sauce.

Mix in crabmeat, season and pour in white sauce. Cook 2 minutes over medium heat.

Spoon mixture over toast, top with cheese and broil 2 minutes in oven.

Camembert Treat

(serves 6-8)

1 SERVING	243 CALORIES	26g CARBOHYDRATE
11g PROTEIN	10g FAT	trace FIBER

1 cup	(250 ml) fine breadcrumbs
3	garlic cloves, smashed and finely chopped
1 tbsp	(15 ml) chopped parsley
1 tsp	(5 ml) celery seed
1 tsp	(5 ml) sesame seed
¼ tsp	(1 ml) paprika
1	small round of Camembert cheese, chilled
½	French baguette, sliced and toasted on both sides
	dash cayenne pepper

Mix breadcrumbs with garlic, parsley and seasonings; set aside.

Remove soft crust from sides of cheese. Lightly scrape top and bottom with knife.

Place cheese in bowl with breadcrumbs and coat. Remove cheese and set on cutting board; flatten with rolling pin.

Turn cheese over, sprinkle with more breadcrumbs and roll again.

Repeat procedure using all breadcrumbs and rolling until cheese is ¼ in (0.65 cm) thick.

Using cookie cutter about the same size as the bread slices, cut out pieces of cheese and set on bread.

Broil 2 minutes in oven.

Serve cold.

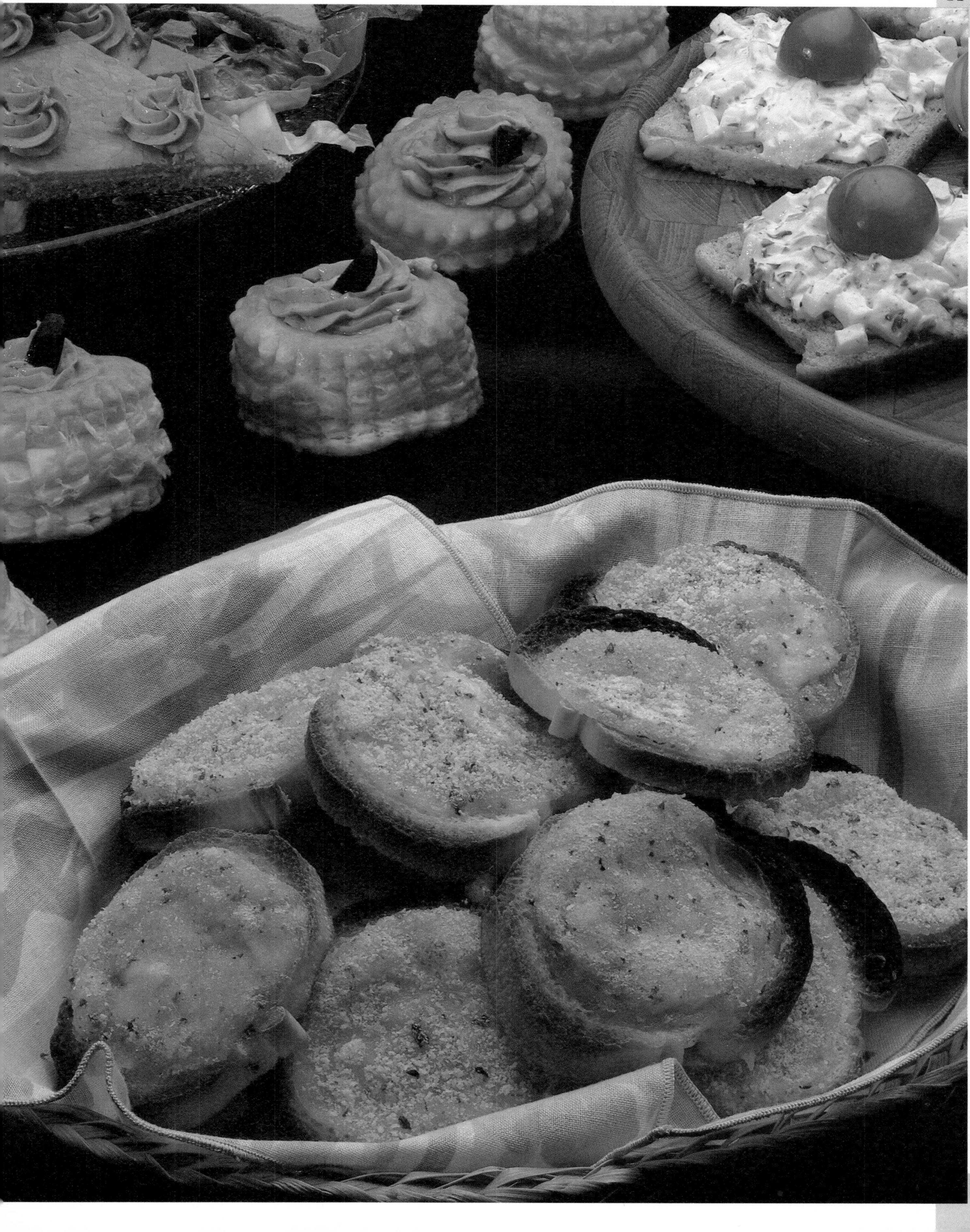

Beef Strips

(serves 8-10)

1 SERVING	314 CALORIES	26g CARBOHYDRATE
19g PROTEIN	15g FAT	trace FIBER

1 tbsp	(15 ml) vegetable oil
1½ lb	(750 g) strip loin steaks, 1 in (2.5 cm) thick, fat trimmed
1	shallot, chopped
1 tbsp	(15 ml) chopped parsley
1 tsp	(5 ml) lemon juice
1 tsp	(5 ml) Worcestershire sauce
1 tbsp	(15 ml) red wine vinegar
2 tbsp	(30 ml) olive oil
3 tbsp	(45 ml) butter
1 tsp	(5 ml) strong mustard
	salt and pepper
	sliced French baguette
	endive leaves for garnish

Heat oil in large frying pan or on nonstick grill. When very hot, add meat and sear 3 minutes over medium-high heat.

Turn meat over, season well and continue searing another 3 to 4 minutes.

Turn meat over again; finish cooking 3 minutes for rare meat.

Remove meat from pan and slice thinly on an angle; place pieces on plate.

Cover meat with shallot, parsley, lemon juice, Worcestershire sauce, vinegar, oil and pepper. Cover loosely with plastic wrap and refrigerate 2 hours.

Drain meat if necessary and set aside.

Mix butter with mustard, spread over bread and toast in oven.

Remove and top with marinated meat. Serve with endive leaves as garnish.

Trim excess fat from meat. **1**

Sear meat a total of 9 to 10 minutes for rare. **2**

3 Remove meat from pan and thinly slice on an angle; place pieces on plate.

4 Cover meat with shallot, parsley, lemon juice, Worcestershire sauce, vinegar, oil and pepper. Cover loosely with plastic wrap and refrigerate 2 hours.

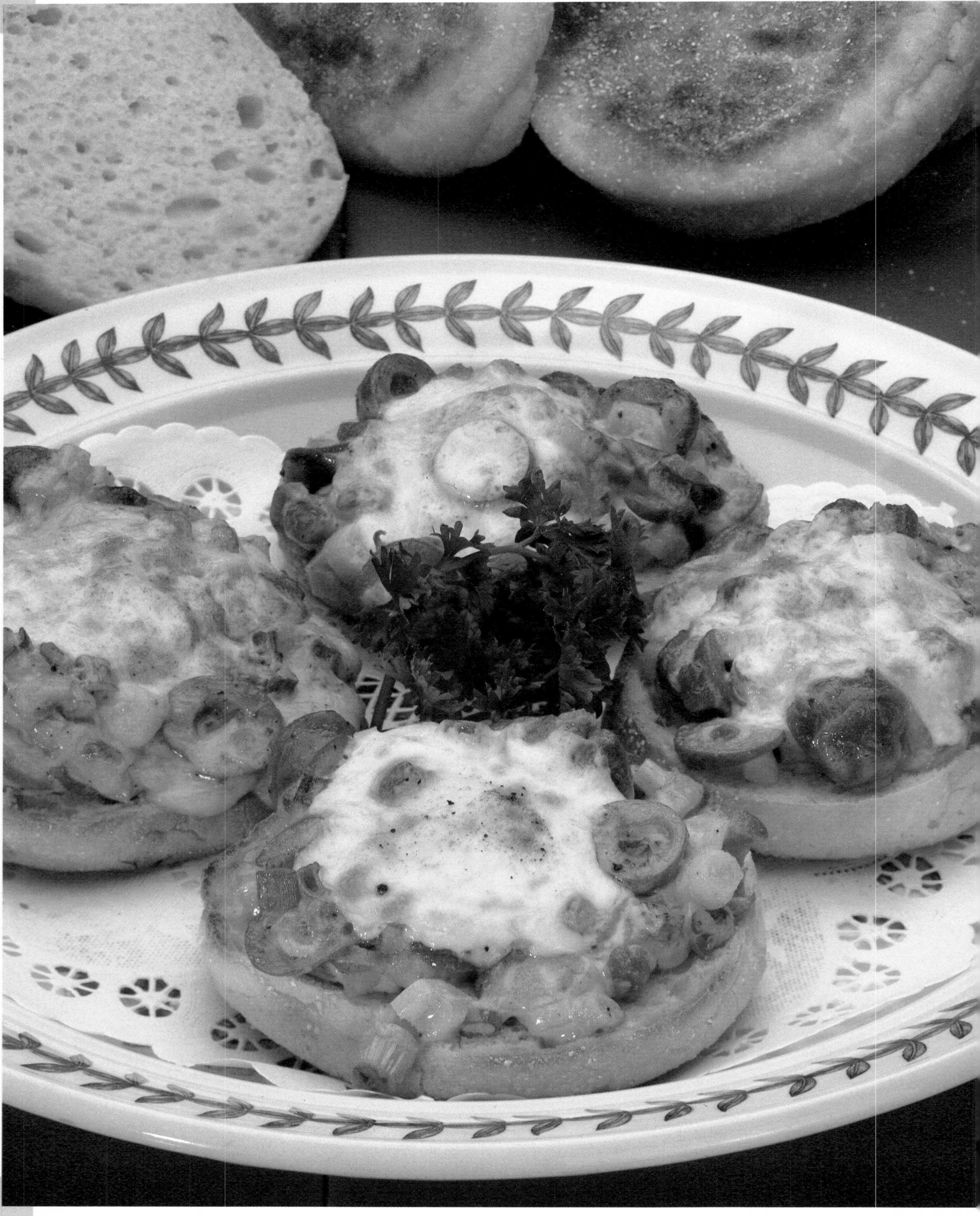

Cheesy Muffin Starter

(serves 4)

1 SERVING	413 CALORIES	25g CARBOHYDRATE
15g PROTEIN	29g FAT	2.0g FIBER

1 cup	(250 ml) stuffed green olives, sliced
4	green onions, chopped
1	celery stalk, chopped
2	slices processed Gruyère cheese, diced
¼ tsp	(1 ml) celery seed
¼ tsp	(1 ml) paprika
3 tbsp	(45 ml) mayonnaise
1 tbsp	(15 ml) Dijon mustard
1 tsp	(5 ml) lemon juice
¼ tsp	(1 ml) Worcestershire sauce
2	English muffins, halved
4	squares mozzarella cheese
	salt and pepper
	more paprika to taste

Place olives, onions, celery, Gruyère cheese, seasonings and mayonnaise in bowl; mix well.

Add mustard, lemon juice and Worcestershire sauce; mix again and correct seasoning.

Set muffin halves on ovenproof platter and top with olive mixture. Cover with mozzarella and dash of paprika.

Broil in oven until melted.

Place olives, onions and celery in bowl.

Add Gruyère cheese, seasonings and mayonnaise; mix well.

Add mustard, lemon juice and Worcestershire sauce; mix again and correct seasoning.

Set muffin halves on ovenproof platter and top with olive mixture. Cover with mozzarella and dash of paprika. Broil in oven until melted.

Ricotta Tomato Bread

(serves 4-6)

1 SERVING	429 CALORIES	58g CARBOHYDRATE
16g PROTEIN	14g FAT	1.0g FIBER

2 tbsp	(30 ml) vegetable oil
1	celery stalk, diced
½	green pepper, chopped
1	onion, chopped
2	garlic cloves, smashed and chopped
¼ tsp	(1 ml) paprika
¼ tsp	(1 ml) chili powder
28 oz	(796 ml) can tomatoes, drained and chopped

3 tbsp	(45 ml) tomato paste
⅓ cup	(75 ml) grated Parmesan cheese
1	French baguette, cut in half lengthwise
½ cup	(125 ml) ricotta cheese salt and pepper

Heat oil in large skillet. Cook celery, green pepper, onion, garlic, paprika and chili powder 4 to 5 minutes over low heat.

Mix in tomatoes and tomato paste; season well. Continue cooking 15 minutes.

Add Parmesan cheese and finish cooking 5 minutes.

Slice each bread half into 3 pieces and toast in oven.

Place bread on cookie sheet or ovenproof platter. Spoon tomato mixture over and top with ricotta cheese.

Broil 3 to 4 minutes or until melted.

Serve immediately.

Cook celery, green pepper, onion, garlic, paprika and chili powder in hot oil for 4 to 5 minutes over low heat.

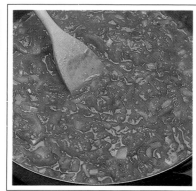

Add Parmesan cheese and finish cooking 5 minutes.

Mix in tomatoes and tomato paste; season well. Continue cooking 15 minutes.

Place toasted bread on cookie sheet and add tomato mixture; top with ricotta cheese and broil in oven.

Vegetable Sandwich Loaf

(serves 6-8)

1 SERVING	323 CALORIES	42g CARBOHYDRATE
9g PROTEIN	13g FAT	trace FIBER

6 oz	(170 g) pepper cream cheese
3 tbsp	(45 ml) sour cream
1 tsp	(5 ml) chopped parsley
¼ tsp	(1 ml) paprika
1	loaf white bread, unsliced
½	English cucumber, thinly sliced
6	radishes, thinly sliced
1	small bunch asparagus, cooked
	salt and pepper

Mix cheese, sour cream, parsley, paprika, salt and pepper together in food processor until smooth.

Using long bread knife, slice off top and bottom crusts of loaf. Continue cutting loaf to obtain 4 slices. See Technique for visual help.

Spread first slice of bread with cheese mixture. Set on large sheet of aluminum foil and layer with cucumbers; season well.

Butter second slice of bread with cheese mixture on both sides and set over cucumbers. Layer radishes on bread and season well.

Butter third slice of bread with cheese mixture on both sides; place on sandwich. Arrange asparagus on bread, trimming to size; season well.

Butter last slice of bread with cheese mixture on one side only. Place, face down, over asparagus and cover sandwich loaf in foil. Use another sheet if needed.

Refrigerate overnight, then slice and serve. If desired trim off crusts before serving.

1 Mix cheese, sour cream, parsley, paprika, salt and pepper together in food processor until smooth.

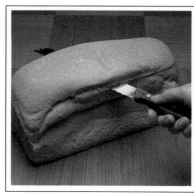

3 Continue cutting loaf to obtain 4 slices.

2 Using long bread knife, slice off top and bottom crusts.

4 Add the last vegetable layer of the sandwich.

Crêpes with Spinach

(serves 4)

1 SERVING	579 CALORIES	35g CARBOHYDRATE
22g PROTEIN	36g FAT	1.0g FIBER

1 cup	(250 ml) all-purpose flour
¼ tsp	(1 ml) salt
¼ tsp	(1 ml) paprika
¼ tsp	(1 ml) ground ginger
½ tsp	(2 ml) celery seed
3	whole eggs
1 cup	(250 ml) beer
3 tbsp	(45 ml) melted butter
½ cup	(125 ml) milk
2	10 oz (284 g) packages spinach, well washed and drained
½ cup	(125 ml) grated Parmesan cheese
¼ cup	(50 ml) olive oil
¼ tsp	(1 ml) nutmeg
½ cup	(125 ml) grated Romano cheese
1 tbsp	(15 ml) melted butter
	extra butter
	salt and pepper

Mix flour, salt, paprika, ginger and celery seed together in bowl.

Whisk in eggs until throughly blended. Add beer and whisk again. Stir in 3 tbsp (45 ml) melted butter.

Pass batter through medium-fine sieve (holes must be large enough for celery seed) into clean bowl.

Pour in milk and mix well. Refrigerate 2 hours uncovered.

Remove batter from refrigerator and mix well. If too thick, add a bit of milk.

Spread small amount of butter on crêpe pan with paper towel. Place pan over medium-high heat and when butter heats wipe off excess with paper towel.

Pour small ladle of batter on tilted crêpe pan and rotate to completely coat bottom. Allow excess batter to drip back into bowl.

Cook crêpe over medium-high heat until brown — about 1 minute. Then using long spatula knife turn crêpe over and cook other side about the same time.

After each crêpe, wipe pan with lightly buttered paper towel. Adjust heat as necessary to maintain an even temperature for all the crêpes.

Set cooked crêpes aside.

Steam spinach 3 minutes. Squeeze out excess liquid by pressing with spoon. Blend 2 minutes in food processor.

Add Parmesan cheese and blend 1 minute; season well.

Add olive oil through top in food processor while it is mixing. Correct seasoning and add nutmeg.

Lay desired amount of crêpes flat on cutting board. Spread puréed spinach over each crêpe but keep some filling for decoration.

Roll crêpes and place on cookie sheet. Sprinkle with Romano cheese and 1 tbsp (15 ml) melted butter. Broil several minutes in oven.

Decorate crêpes with reserved spinach filling.

Mix flour, salt, paprika, ginger and celery seed together in bowl.

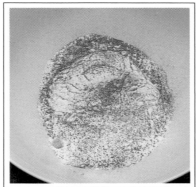

Whisk in eggs until thoroughly blended.

Cook crêpe over medium-high heat until brown — about 1 minute. Then using long spatula knife turn crêpe over.

Cook other side of crêpe about the same length of time.

Crab Vol-au-Vent

(serves 4-6)

1 SERVING	537 CALORIES	26g CARBOHYDRATE
16g PROTEIN	41g FAT	trace FIBER

3 tbsp	(45 ml) butter
1	shallot, chopped
½	celery stalk, chopped
8	large mushrooms, chopped
¼ tsp	(1 ml) anise
¼ tsp	(1 ml) paprika
2 tbsp	(30 ml) flour
1½ cups	(375 ml) hot milk
1 tsp	(5 ml) cumin
5 oz	(142 g) can snow crabmeat, drained
12	small vol-au-vent, cooked
1 cup	(250 ml) grated cheddar cheese
	salt and pepper

Heat butter in large skillet. Cook shallot 1 minute.

Add celery, mushrooms, anise, paprika and season well. Continue cooking 2 to 3 minutes over medium heat.

Mix in flour and cook 2 minutes over medium-low heat.

Add milk, mix well and bring to boil. Add cumin and continue cooking 4 to 5 minutes over low heat.

Stir in crab and finish cooking 2 minutes over low heat.

Spoon crab mixture into vol-au-vent set on ovenproof platter. Top with cheese and broil in oven until melted.

Decorate with olives if desired.

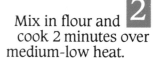
Add celery mushrooms, anise, paprika, salt and pepper to shallot in skillet. Continue cooking 2 to 3 minutes.

Add milk, mix well and bring to boil. Add cumin and continue cooking 4 to 5 minutes over low heat.

Mix in flour and cook 2 minutes over medium-low heat.

Stir in crab and finish cooking 2 minutes over low heat.

Scallops in Pastry Shells

(serves 4-6)

1 SERVING	514 CALORIES	27g CARBOHYDRATE
16g PROTEIN	34g FAT	trace FIBER

1 tbsp	(15 ml) butter
½ lb	(250 g) mushrooms, quartered
½ cup	(125 ml) dry white wine
1 tbsp	(15 ml) chopped shallot
1 tbsp	(15 ml) chopped parsley
½ lb	(250 g) scallops, halved
¾ cup	(175 ml) thick white sauce, hot
12	small vol-au-vent or tartlets, cooked and cooled
½ cup	(125 ml) grated Parmesan cheese
	salt and pepper

Heat butter in skillet. Add mushrooms, wine, shallot and parsley; cook 3 to 4 minutes over medium-high heat.

Stir in scallops and continue cooking 2 minutes over medium heat.

Pour in white sauce, season and cook 1 minute.

Place pastry shells on ovenproof platter and fill with scallop mixture. Top with cheese and broil 2 to 3 minutes in oven.

Serve on lettuce leaves if desired.

Mushroom Vol-au-Vent

(serves 4)

1 SERVING	692 CALORIES	27g CARBOHYDRATE
16g PROTEIN	57g FAT	0.5g FIBER

10 oz	(284 g) fine liver pâté
2 tbsp	(30 ml) sour cream
1 tbsp	(15 ml) Dijon mustard
2 tbsp	(30 ml) butter
1	shallot, chopped
1	garlic clove, smashed and chopped
½ lb	(250 g) mushrooms, finely chopped
3 tbsp	(45 ml) ricotta cheese
12	small vol-au-vent, cooked
	dash paprika
	salt and pepper

Blend pâté, sour cream and mustard together in food processor; set aside.

Heat butter in saucepan. Cook shallot and garlic 2 minutes over medium heat.

Add mushrooms and paprika; season well. Continue cooking 4 to 5 minutes.

Stir in cheese, correct seasoning and cook 2 minutes over low heat. Remove saucepan from heat and set aside to cool.

Fill vol-au-vent with cold mushroom mixture and arrange on serving platter.

Spoon pâté mixture into pastry bag fitted with plain nozzle. Decorate the tops of vol-au-vent. Keep leftover pâté for spreading on crackers.

Garnish with watercress and quartered black olives if desired.

Asparagus Pastry Bites

(serves 8-10)

1 SERVING	558 CALORIES	46g CARBOHYDRATE
9g PROTEIN	38g FAT	0.7g FIBER

3 tbsp	(45 ml) butter
1 tbsp	(15 ml) green peppercorns, mashed
1	red pepper, diced
1	green onion, sliced
1 tsp	(5 ml) chopped jalapeno pepper
3 tbsp	(45 ml) flour
1½ cups	(375 ml) hot milk
1 tsp	(5 ml) fennel seed
2	bunches asparagus, tips cooked and diced
24	tartlets, cooked and cooled
½ cup	(125 ml) grated cheddar cheese
	salt and pepper

Heat butter in skillet. Cook mashed peppercorns, red pepper, green onion and jalapeno pepper 3 minutes over medium heat.

Mix in flour and continue cooking 2 minutes over low heat.

Pour in milk, add fennel seed and season well. Mix and continue cooking 5 to 6 minutes over low heat.

Stir in asparagus, season and simmer 2 minutes.

Place tartlets on ovenproof platter and fill with asparagus mixture. Top with cheese and broil in oven until melted.

Serve on a bed of alfalfa sprouts if desired.

Vegetable Tartlets

(serves 4)

1 SERVING	569 CALORIES	40g CARBOHYDRATE
10g PROTEIN	40g FAT	0.6g FIBER

2 tbsp	(30 ml) butter
2	shallots, finely chopped
1	garlic clove, smashed and chopped
½ lb	(250 g) mushrooms, chopped
1 cup	(250 ml) white sauce, heated
8	tartlets, cooked
¼ cup	(50 ml) grated Parmesan cheese
	salt and pepper
	dash nutmeg

Heat butter in saucepan. Cook shallots and garlic 2 minutes over low heat.

Season and add mushrooms and nutmeg; cook 4 to 5 minutes over medium-high heat.

Pour in white sauce and continue cooking 2 to 3 minutes over medium heat.

Spoon mixture into tartlets set on cookie sheet. Add cheese and broil 3 minutes in oven.

Shrimp and Mushroom Tartlets

(serves 4)

1 SERVING	713 CALORIES	43g CARBOHYDRATE
31g PROTEIN	47g FAT	0.7g FIBER

2 tbsp	(30 ml) butter
18	mushrooms, diced
1	shallot, chopped
1 tbsp	(15 ml) curry powder
¾ lb	(375 g) cooked shrimp, diced
1½ cups	(375 ml) white sauce, heated
8	tartlets, cooked
½ cup	(125 ml) grated Gruyère cheese
	salt and pepper

Heat butter in frying pan over medium heat. Cook mushrooms and shallot 4 minutes.

Season and add curry powder and shrimp; continue cooking 1 minute.

Pour in sauce, mix well and cook 1 minute.

Fill tartlets with mixture and top with cheese. Broil 2 to 3 minutes in oven and serve.

Spinach-Stuffed Mushrooms

(serves 6-8)

1 SERVING	233 CALORIES	14g CARBOHYDRATE
12g PROTEIN	16g FAT	1.0g FIBER

3 tbsp	(45 ml) butter
1 lb	(500 g) spinach, cooked, chopped and well drained
2	garlic cloves, smashed and chopped
3 tbsp	(45 ml) flour
1½ cups	(375 ml) hot milk
¼ tsp	(1 ml) nutmeg
1¼ cups	(300 ml) grated mozzarella cheese
2 lb	(900 g) mushroom caps, cleaned
2 tbsp	(30 ml) melted butter
	salt and pepper
	juice ½ limon
	dash paprika

Place 3 tbsp (45 ml) butter in large skillet and heat. When melted, add spinach and garlic; cook 3 to 4 minutes over medium-high heat.

Mix in flour and continue cooking 2 to 3 minutes over low heat while mixing constantly.

Pour in milk and season with nutmeg, salt and pepper; mix well. Add ½ cup (125 ml) cheese, mix and cook 2 to 3 minutes over medium heat.

Set mushroom caps on ovenproof serving platter; sprinkle with lemon juice, paprika and 2 tbsp (30 ml) melted butter. Broil 5 minutes in oven.

Fill mushroom caps with spinach stuffing and top with remaining cheese. Finish broiling about 5 minutes or until cheese starts to brown.

Vegetable Artichoke Bottoms

(serves 4)

1 SERVING	223 CALORIES	20g CARBOHYDRATE
5g PROTEIN	15g FAT	.4g FIBER

8	artichoke bottoms
1 tbsp	(15 ml) lemon juice
2 tbsp	(30 ml) olive oil
¼ tsp	(1 ml) Tabasco sauce
1	green pepper, diced small
1	carrot, pared and diced small
1	yellow pepper, diced small
⅓	celery stalk, diced small
3 tbsp	(45 ml) mayonnaise
¼ tsp	(1 ml) Worcestershire sauce
	salt and pepper

Place artichoke bottoms in bowl; sprinkle with lemon juice, oil, Tabasco sauce, salt and pepper. Marinate 30 minutes.

Place remaining vegetables in another bowl. Add mayonnaise, Worcestershire sauce, salt and pepper; mix well.

Fill artichoke bottoms with vegetable mixture and serve.

Fancy Artichoke Bottoms

(serves 4)

1 SERVING	378 CALORIES	25g CARBOHYDRATE
18g PROTEIN	26g FAT	5.0g FIBER

12	stuffed green olives, chopped
12	pitted black olives, chopped
4 oz	(113 g) can small shrimp, drained and rinsed
1 tsp	(5 ml) chopped parsley
1	celery stalk, chopped
½	pickled banana pepper, chopped
3 tbsp	(45 ml) mayonnaise
¼ cup	(50 ml) water
1 tbsp	(15 ml) butter
10	artichoke bottoms
10	small squares mozzarella cheese
	salt and pepper
	juice ½ lemon

Mix both olives, shrimp, parsley, celery, banana pepper and mayonnaise together. Correct seasoning and add extra mayonnaise if desired.

Place water, butter, artichoke bottoms and lemon juice in saucepan; bring to boil. Remove saucepan from heat and let stand 2 to 3 minutes on counter.

Remove artichoke bottoms from pan and transfer to ovenproof serving platter. Fill each with shrimp stuffing and top with squares of mozzarella cheese.

Broil about 2 to 3 minutes in oven or until cheese melts. If desired sprinkle with paprika for decoration.

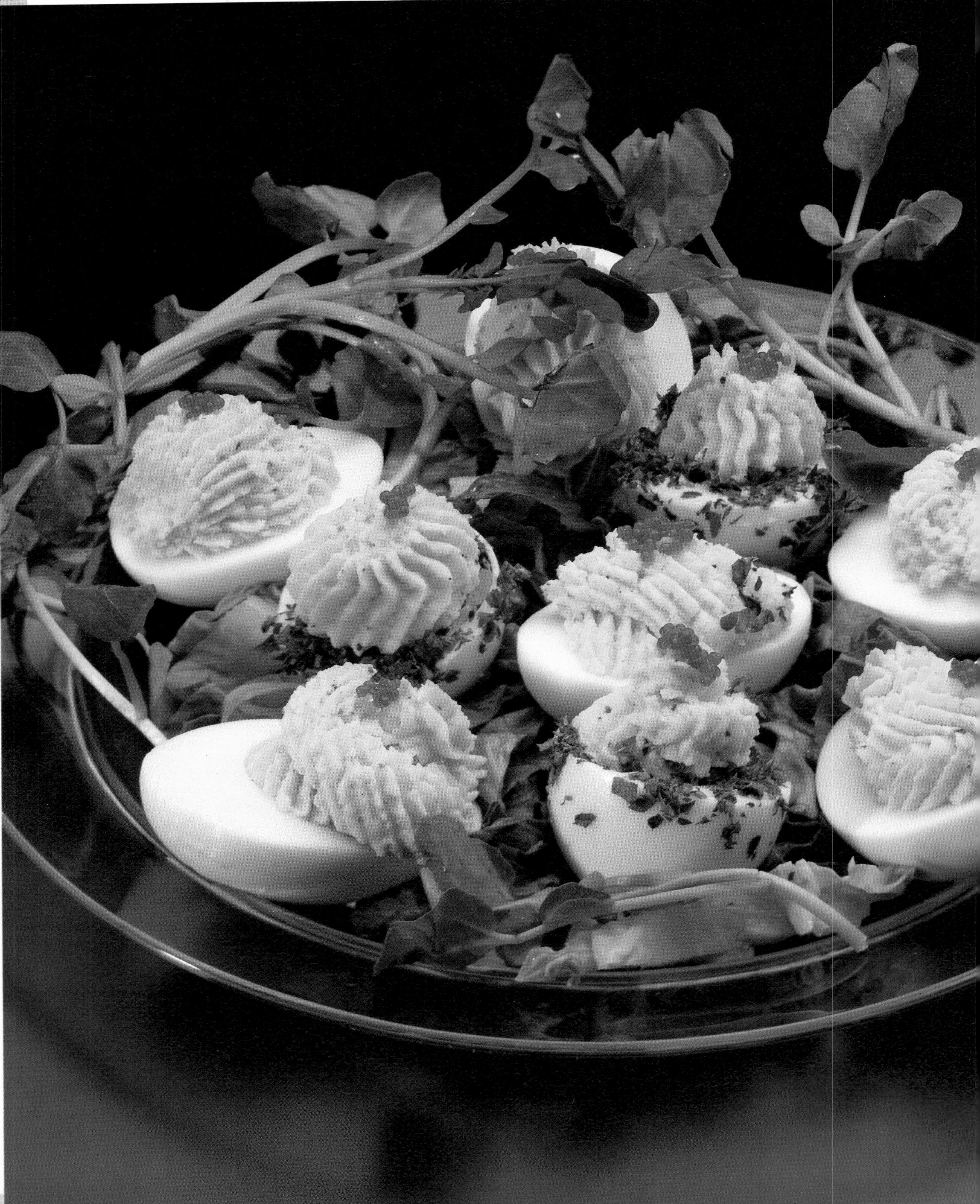

Shrimp-Stuffed Eggs

(serves 6)

1 SERVING	280 CALORIES	1g CARBOHYDRATE
16g PROTEIN	23g FAT	-- FIBER

6	large eggs
4 oz	(113 g) can small shrimp, drained and rinsed
1 tsp	(5 ml) chopped parsley
2 tbsp	(30 ml) soft butter
3 tbsp	(45 ml) mayonnaise
¼ tsp	(1 ml) paprika
	few drops lemon juice
	few drops Worcestershire sauce
	salt and pepper
	extra chopped parsley
	extra mayonnaise

Cook eggs 10 minutes in gently boiling water. When cooked, drain and cool under running water for at least 3 to 4 minutes.

Peel eggs and cut in half, either lengthwise or widthwise.

Carefully remove yolks and place in sieve set over bowl. Force through with pestle and be sure to scrape the bottom of sieve to gather all the yolks. Set aside in bowl.

Pat shrimp dry with paper towel. Place in food processor along with parsley; purée.

Transfer shrimp to bowl containing sieved yolks. Add butter and mix well.

Stir in mayonnaise until well incorporated. Season with paprika, lemon juice, Worcestershire sauce, salt and pepper. Mix well with spatula.

Arrange the egg white halves on plate. Decorate several by coating tops in mayonnaise then dipping in chopped parsley.

Spoon shrimp filling into pastry bag fitted with large star nozzle. Force into egg white halves and, if desired, decorate with a bit of caviar.

1 After eggs have cooled for at least 3 to 4 minutes in cold water, peel away shells.

3 With pestle, force egg yolks through sieve into bowl.

2 Cut eggs in half, either lengthwise or widthwise.

4 Purée shrimp with parsley in food processor.

Vegetables with Cheese Dip

(serves 6-8)

1 SERVING	255 CALORIES	29g CARBOHYDRATE
16g PROTEIN	12g FAT	4.0g FIBER

6 oz	(170 g) blue cheese, in chunks
1 tsp	(5 ml) Worcestershire sauce
½ cup	(125 ml) sour cream
¼ tsp	(1 ml) paprika
2 tbsp	(30 ml) caviar
1	head broccoli, flowerets blanched
2	carrots, pared, cut in sticks, and blanched if desired
6	green onion sticks
1	zucchini, peeled and in sticks
1	apple, cored and in wedges
1	celery stalk, in sticks
1	green pepper, sliced
	salt and pepper
	few leaves Boston lettuce

Place cheese and Worcestershire sauce in food processor; blend until puréed.

Add sour cream and paprika; continue blending until very smooth. Use spatula several times to clean sides of bowl.

Add caviar and blend another 30 seconds. Season with some salt and plenty of pepper.

Arrange lettuce leaves in middle of large serving platter. Spoon cheese dip over leaves and surround with vegetable and apple sticks.

Although the broccoli should be blanched it is a matter of taste as to whether or not you blanch the carrots.

Place cheese and Worcestershire sauce in food processor; blend until puréed.

Add sour cream and paprika; continue blending until very smooth. Use spatula several times to clean sides of bowl.

Add caviar and blend another 30 seconds. Season with some salt and plenty of pepper.

Spicy Dip for Vegetables

(serves 4)

1 RECIPE	948 CALORIES	13g CARBOHYDRATE
21g PROTEIN	92g FAT	1.0g FIBER

1 tsp	(5 ml) strong mustard
½ lb	(250 g) cream cheese
½ cup	(125 ml) finely chopped red pepper
½ tsp	(2 ml) cumin
1	garlic clove, smashed and chopped
1 tbsp	(15 ml) sour cream
1 tsp	(5 ml) finely chopped chives
¼ tsp	(1 ml) paprika
¼ tsp	(1 ml) celery seed
	few drops lemon juice
	salt and pepper
	assorted vegetable sticks

Blend mustard and cream cheese in food processor until smooth.

Add red pepper, cumin, garlic and sour cream; mix well.

Stir in chives, paprika, celery seed, lemon juice; season very well and blend together.

Serve with assorted vegetable sticks.

Versatile Cheese Dip

(serves 4)

1 RECIPE	1997 CALORIES	6g CARBOHYDRATE
65g PROTEIN	192g FAT	-- FIBER

½ lb	(250 g) strong cheddar cheese
¼ cup	(50 ml) sour cream
¼ lb	(125 g) soft butter
1 tbsp	(15 ml) finely chopped chives
1 tbsp	(15 ml) finely chopped parsley
	salt and pepper
	few drops Tabasco sauce
	few drops Worcestershire sauce
	assorted crackers

Blend cheese in food processor until quite smooth.

Add sour cream and butter; mix again until incorporated.

Add chives, parsley, salt, pepper, Tabasco and Worcestershire; blend again.

Serve dip on crackers.

Chicken Liver Appetizer

(serves 4)

1 SERVING	312 CALORIES	9g CARBOHYDRATE
34g PROTEIN	14g FAT	0.6g FIBER

1	head Boston lettuce
2 tbsp	(30 ml) olive oil
1 lb	(500 g) fresh chicken livers, cleaned, halved and fat trimmed
2	garlic cloves, smashed and chopped
1	onion, thinly sliced
3	anchovy filets, chopped
2 tbsp	(30 ml) capers
¼ tsp	(1 ml) sage
1½ cups	(375 ml) chicken stock, heated
1 tbsp	(15 ml) cornstarch
3 tbsp	(45 ml) cold water
	salt and pepper

Wash and dry lettuce; arrange leaves like baskets on four individual plates. Set aside.

Heat oil in frying pan. Cook livers, garlic and onion 3 to 4 minutes over medium heat; season well.

Stir in anchovies, capers and sage; continue cooking 1 minute.

Pour in chicken stock and bring to boil. Mix cornstarch with water; incorporate into sauce and cook 1 minute over low heat.

Spoon mixture into lettuce baskets and serve immediately.

DESSERTS

Desserts

«If I had to live the rest of my life as a food, I would choose to be a lone strawberry, covered ever so delicately in smooth chocolate sauce, set atop the highest mound of swirled vanilla ice cream surrounded by a tiny sea of colored sprinkles.»

Anonymous

It's a fact that no matter how hard we try to resist the temptation, desserts in their many forms and disguises win the tug-of-war almost every time!

For some it may be the cool elegance of a parfait, assembled so neatly in a tall, frosty glass that makes their eyes sparkle. For others, a generous portion of rich chocolate cake smothered in fluffy, cognac-laced whipped cream might be the ultimate reward. Whatever your enthusiasm, this collection of fruit and dessert recipes will surpass anything your palate has experienced before. You will discover the natural goodness of exotic fruit in recipes such as Mango Mousse and Passion Fruit Cream Dessert, and devour such favorites as Shortbread Cookies and Almond Brownies. And for those who relish a mysterious tinge to their cookery, you can try Apple Galette and Cherry Clafoutis.

Before reading on, remember one thing: desserts are not just another course — they are extra-special and need your complete concentration. So put your whole heart into the preparation of these recipes and no cutting corners — they will turn out every bit as sumptuous as you imagined!

Chocolate Frosting

¼ cup (50 ml)	248 CALORIES	35g CARBOHYDRATE
2g PROTEIN	10g FAT	0.2g FIBER

4 oz	(125 g) unsweetened chocolate
2¼ cups	(550 ml) icing sugar
3 tbsp	(45 ml) hot rum
2	egg yolks
¼ cup	(50 ml) softened unsalted butter

Place chocolate in stainless steel bowl, set over saucepan half-filled with boiling water. Melt.

Remove bowl from heat and add icing sugar. Incorporate using electric beater.

Add hot rum and mix well with spatula.

Add egg yolks, one at a time, mixing well between each.

Add butter and mix very well with spatula or electric beater if necessary. Consistency should be smooth.

When cool, spread frosting over almost any type of cake.

Chocolate Sundae

(serves 4)

1 SERVING	598 CALORIES	55g CARBOHYDRATE
10g PROTEIN	37g FAT	0.9g FIBER

4 oz	(125 g) unsweetened chocolate
½ cup	(125 ml) granulated sugar
1 tbsp	(15 ml) maple syrup
¼ cup	(50 ml) water
2 tbsp	(30 ml) rum
½ cup	(125 ml) heavy cream
	vanilla ice cream
	chopped walnuts

Place chocolate in stainless steel bowl set over saucepan half-filled with boiling water and melt.

Remove bowl from heat and set aside.

Place sugar, maple syrup and water in saucepan. Bring to boil and continue cooking 2-3 minutes over medium heat.

Remove saucepan from heat and let cool slightly.

When sugar-syrup mixture is lukewarm, add rum and mix well.

Add melted chocolate and mix well. Slowly pour in cream while whisking constantly.

Pour chocolate sauce into bowl and refrigerate until cold.

Serve with vanilla ice cream and decorate with chopped walnuts.

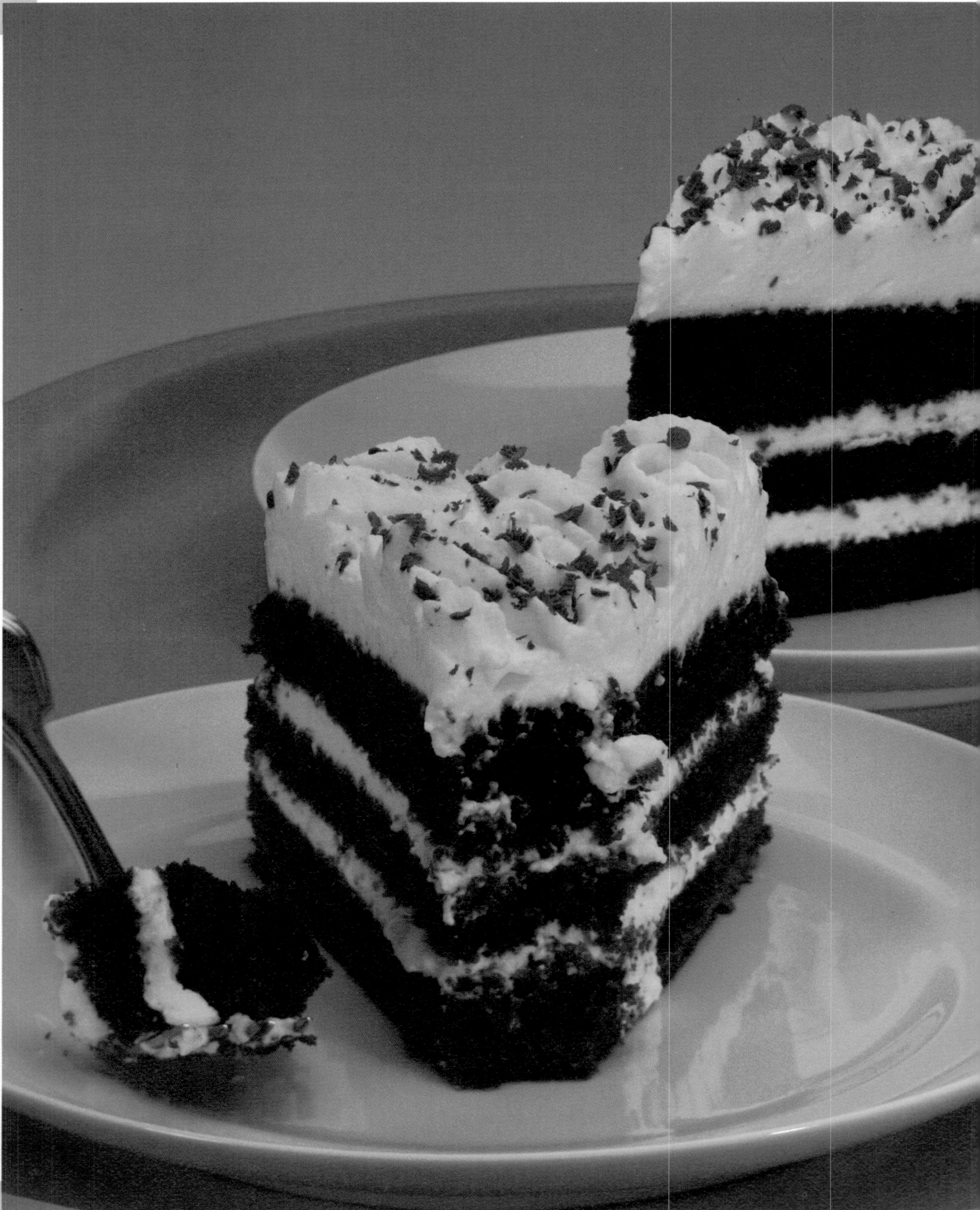

Chocolate Layer Cake

(serves 8-10)

1 SERVING	479 CALORIES	57g CARBOHYDRATE
7g PROTEIN	25g FAT	0.4g FIBER

2 cups	(500 ml) pastry flour
1¾ cups	(425 ml) granulated sugar
⅔ cup	(150 ml) unsweetened cocoa
1 tbsp	(15 ml) baking soda
1 tsp	(5 ml) baking powder
¾ cup	(175 ml) all-vegetable shortening
1 cup	(250 ml) milk
3	eggs
	pinch salt
	whipped cream
	shaved chocolate

Preheat oven to 325°F (160°C). Butter 10 inch (25 cm) spring-form cake pan.

Sift flour, sugar, cocoa, baking soda, baking powder and salt into large bowl.

Add shortening and incorporate with pastry blender.

Pour in milk and beat well with electric beater until batter is smooth.

Add eggs, one at a time, beating 30 seconds after each addition.

Pour batter into prepared cake pan and bake 65 minutes or until toothpick inserted comes out clean.

When cake is cooked, remove from oven and let cool 10-15 minutes in pan.

Carefully unmold and let cool completely on wire rack at room temperature.

Slice cake into two or three layers and ice with whipped cream. Decorate with shaved chocolate.

Chocolate Mousse

(serves 4-6)

1 SERVING	376 CALORIES	9g CARBOHYDRATE
9g PROTEIN	34g FAT	0.5g FIBER

6 oz	(170 g) semi-sweet chocolate
3 tbsp	(45 ml) unsalted butter
¼ cup	(50 ml) water
4	egg yolks
2 tbsp	(30 ml) Tia Maria liqueur
4	egg whites, beaten stiff
½ cup	(125 ml) heavy cream, whipped
	shaved chocolate for decoration

Place chocolate, butter and water in saucepan and cook over low heat to melt. Mix constantly with wooden spoon.

Remove from heat and transfer chocolate to bowl.

Add egg yolks, one at a time, mixing between additions with whisk.

Add Tia Maria and continue whisking several seconds.

Incorporate egg whites using spatula, being careful not to overmix.

Add whipped cream and incorporate with spatula.

Mix well with whisk for several seconds.

Pour into glass bowls and refrigerate 4 hours before serving. Decorate with shaved chocolate.

Chocolate Berry Mousse

(serves 4-6)

1 SERVING	321 CALORIES	24g CARBOHYDRATE
3g PROTEIN	24g FAT	0.5g FIBER

3	squares semi-sweet chocolate
1	egg
½ cup	(125 ml) puréed strawberries
1 cup	(250 ml) hot heavy cream
3	egg whites
½ cup	(125 ml) sugar

Melt chocolate in stainless steel bowl set over saucepan half-filled with hot water, placed over medium heat.

Remove bowl from pan; mix in whole egg with whisk.

Add puréed strawberries and mix well. Pour into food processor and blend 1 minute.

Blend in hot cream and continue processing until well incorporated. Refrigerate to cool.

Beat egg whites until stiff. Slowly add sugar while beating until incorporated.

Fold egg whites into chilled mousse batter and spoon into glass dishes.

Refrigerate before serving.

Strawberry and Raspberry Mousse

(serves 6-8)

1 SERVING	226 CALORIES	28g CARBOHYDRATE
4g PROTEIN	11g FAT	1.6g FIBER

1½	small envelopes unflavored gelatine
¼ cup	(50 ml) hot water
⅔ cup	(150 ml) granulated sugar
3 tbsp	(45 ml) maple syrup
½ cup	(125 ml) boiling water
2 cups	(500 ml) fresh strawberries, hulled
1 cup	(250 ml) fresh raspberries
1 tbsp	(15 ml) grated lemon rind
5	egg whites
1 cup	(250 ml) heavy cream, whipped

Grease 8 cup (2 L) soufflé mold with oil.

Sprinkle gelatine over ¼ cup (50 ml) hot water placed in small bowl; set aside.

Place half of sugar, maple syrup and boiling water in saucepan. Bring to boil and continue cooking 2 minutes over medium heat.

Stir in both fruits and lemon rind; continue cooking 3 minutes.

Transfer contents to food processor and purée.

Replace mixture in saucepan and mix in gelatine; cook 1 minute.

Pour fruit mixture into bowl and refrigerate.

When fruit mixture starts to set, begin preparing egg whites by placing them in bowl.

Beat with electric beater until they peak. Add remaining sugar and continue beating 30 seconds.

Fold into fruit mixture using spatula.

Incorporate whipped cream and pour mixture into prepared mold. Refrigerate 8 hours.

Unmold and serve with a fruit sauce.

Strawberry Omelet

(serves 4)

1 SERVING	369 CALORIES	28g CARBOHYDRATE
13g PROTEIN	23g FAT	1.8g FIBER

2 cups	(500 ml) strawberries, hulled and sliced in 3
4 tbsp	(60 ml) butter
3 tbsp	(45 ml) sugar
1 cup	(250 ml) orange juice
2 tsp	(10 ml) cornstarch
3 tbsp	(45 ml) cold water
8	eggs, well beaten

Set strawberries aside in bowl.

Heat half of butter in frying pan. Add 2 tbsp (30 ml) sugar and cook 2 minutes over high heat while stirring constantly.

Continue stirring, pour in orange juice and bring to boil. Cook 2 more minutes over high heat.

Mix cornstarch with water; stir into sauce. Cook 1 minute over high heat, stirring occasionally.

Pour over strawberries and let stand 15 minutes.

Heat remaining butter in large nonstick frying pan or omelet pan. When hot, pour in eggs and cook 30 seconds over high heat while mixing with fork.

Continue cooking another 30 seconds or until top is set.

Add half of strawberries and cook another 20 seconds.

Carefully roll omelet while tilting pan, then turn onto ovenproof serving platter.

Sprinkle with remaining sugar and broil several minutes in oven.

Meanwhile, heat remaining strawberries in small saucepan.

When ready to serve, pour strawberries over omelet and garnish with shredded coconut if desired.

Using spatula, **1** cream together the butter and brown sugar.

3 Add second egg and 2 tbsp (30 ml) of flour to bowl; beat well with electric beater.

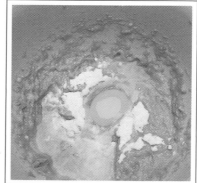

Add first **2** egg and beat well with electric beater.

4 Add last egg, flour and beat again. Pour in coffee and rum; beat well. Pour in cream, beat and add cherries.

Cherry Clafoutis

(serves 4-6)

1 SERVING	362 CALORIES	42g CARBOHYDRATE
6g PROTEIN	19g FAT	0.1g FIBER

¼ cup	(50 ml) softened butter
½ cup	(125 ml) brown sugar
3	eggs
½ cup	(125 ml) all-purpose flour
1 tsp	(5 ml) baking powder
¼ cup	(50 ml) strong black coffee
2 tbsp	(30 ml) rum
1 cup	(250 ml) light cream
14 oz	(398 ml) can pitted Bing cherries, well drained
1 tbsp	(15 ml) granulated sugar
	whipped cream

Preheat oven to 350°F (180°C). Butter 10 inch (25 cm) glass pie plate.

Place butter and brown sugar in bowl; using spatula cream together.

Add first egg and beat well with electric beater.

Sift flour and baking powder together.

Add second egg and 2 tbsp (30 ml) of flour to bowl; beat well with electric beater.

Add last egg and rest of flour; beat again.

Pour in coffee and rum; beat well. Pour in cream, beat and add cherries.

Pour batter into prepared pie plate; bake 45-50 minutes or until toothpick inserted comes out clean.

About 5 minutes before clafoutis is cooked, sprinkle with a bit of granulated sugar and resume cooking.

Serve warm with whipped cream.

Bavarian Cream with Cherries

(serves 6-8)

1 SERVING	260 CALORIES	22g CARBOHYDRATE
5g PROTEIN	17g FAT	0.3g FIBER

6	egg yolks
½ cup	(125 ml) sugar
2 cups	(500 ml) hot milk
1 tbsp	(15 ml) vanilla
2 tbsp	(30 ml) gelatine
¼ cup	(50 ml) cold water
1 cup	(250 ml) heavy cream
2 cups	(500 ml) pitted cherries

Place egg yolks and sugar in stainless steel bowl. Mix together with electric beater for 2 minutes.

Add hot milk and vanilla; mix well to incorporate.

Have ready a saucepan filled with hot water placed over medium heat. Set bowl over saucepan and cook cream until it coats the back of a spoon. Stir constantly.

Remove bowl from saucepan and set aside. Dilute gelatine in cold water; let stand 2 minutes.

Incorporate diluted gelatine into cooked cream. Set bowl over larger bowl filled with ice water.

As soon as the cream mixture starts to set, whip the heavy cream.

Incorporate cherries, then whipping cream into gelling mixture. Pour into oiled mold and refrigerate overnight.

Cottage Sundaes

(serves 4)

1 SERVING	305 CALORIES	38g CARBOHYDRATE
20g PROTEIN	8g FAT	0.9g FIBER

¾ lb	(375 g) pitted cherries
¼ cup	(50 ml) sugar
¼ cup	(50 ml) water
1 tbsp	(15 ml) grated lemon rind
1 tsp	(5 ml) cornstarch
2 tbsp	(30 ml) cold water
2½ cups	(625 ml) cottage cheese
	whipped cream for topping
	maraschino cherries for decoration

Place cherries, sugar, ¼ cup (50 ml) water and lemon rind in saucepan. Cover and cook 2 to 3 minutes over medium heat, stirring occasionally.

Mix cornstarch with 2 tbsp (30 ml) water; stir into cherry sauce and continue cooking 1 minute. Remove pan from heat and let cool.

To build sundaes, alternate cherry sauce and cottage cheese in tall dessert glasses.

Top with whipped cream and decorate with maraschino cherries if desired.

Pastry Cream

¼ cup (50 ml)	81 CALORIES	8g CARBOHYDRATE
3g PROTEIN	4g FAT	0g FIBER

4	egg yolks
¼ cup	(50 ml) granulated sugar
4 tbsp	(60 ml) flour
2 cups	(500 ml) hot milk
2 tbsp	(30 ml) slivered almonds

Place egg yolks in bowl. Add sugar and beat well with whisk.

Add flour, mix with whisk, and pour in milk. Continue mixing until well incorporated.

Stir in almonds and pour mixture into saucepan. Cook over medium heat, stirring constantly, until mixture reaches boiling point.

Continue cooking 2 minutes or until cream starts to thicken.

Pour cream into bowl and let cool slightly. Cover with plastic wrap (it must touch surface of cream) and refrigerate until cold.

Use this pastry cream recipe in a variety of dessert dishes.

Pears with Pastry Cream

(serves 6)

1 SERVING	179 CALORIES	36g CARBOHYDRATE
6g PROTEIN	1g FAT	4.8g FIBER

4 cups	(1 L) water
1½ cups	(375 ml) granulated sugar
1 tbsp	(15 ml) lemon juice
2 tbsp	(30 ml) light rum
6	pears, cored and peeled
1½ cups	(375 ml) pastry cream
4	egg whites, beaten stiff
¼ cup	(50 ml) hot rum

Place water, sugar, lemon juice and light rum in saucepan; bring to boil and continue cooking 4 minutes over medium heat.

Add whole pears and reduce heat. Cook 6 to 7 minutes over low heat.

Remove saucepan from heat and let pears cool in syrup.

Pour pastry cream into ovenproof baking dish. Arrange pears in cream and decorate sides of dish with beaten egg whites. It is best to use pastry bag and nozzle for this.

Broil 2 minutes or until lightly browned.

Remove from oven, pour in hot rum and flambé. Serve immediately.

Sugared Pears

(serves 4)

1 SERVING	514 CALORIES	87g CARBOHYDRATE
3g PROTEIN	17g FAT	7.2g FIBER

½ cup	(125 ml) sugar
2 cups	(500 ml) water
½ cup	(125 ml) orange juice
4	large pears, cored, peeled and halved
1 tbsp	(15 ml) cornstarch
3 tbsp	(45 ml) cold water
3 tbsp	(45 ml) shredded coconut
1 cup	(250 ml) crushed macaroons
1 tbsp	(15 ml) butter

Place sugar, 2 cups (500 ml) water and orange juice in saucepan. Bring to boil over medium heat and continue cooking 3 to 4 minutes.

Add pears and cook 3 minutes over low heat.

Remove saucepan from heat and let pears stand in syrup 5 to 6 minutes.

Remove pears from saucepan and place in baking dish; set aside.

Replace saucepan of syrup on stove; cook 4 to 5 minutes over high heat.

Mix cornstarch with 3 tbsp (45 ml) cold water; stir into syrup and continue cooking 1 minute over low heat.

Pour half of syrup over pears. Top with coconut and macaroons; dot with butter. Broil 3 minutes in oven.

Orange Pears

(serves 4)

1 SERVING	181 CALORIES	42g CARBOHYDRATE
0g PROTEIN	0g FAT	4.7g FIBER

½ cup	(125 ml) sugar
2½ cups	(625 ml) water
1 tsp	(5 ml) vanilla
4	Bartlett pears
½ cup	(125 ml) orange juice
2 tbsp	(30 ml) grated orange rind
1 tsp	(5 ml) cornstarch
2 tbsp	(30 ml) cold water
2 tbsp	(30 ml) orange liqueur

Place sugar, 2½ cups (625 ml) water and vanilla in saucepan. Bring to boil.

Meanwhile, carefully core pears without removing stem. Peel and place pears in syrup mixture in saucepan.

Cook 4 to 5 minutes over low heat. Remove saucepan from heat and let pears cool in syrup.

Remove pears and set on serving platter; set aside.

Remove 1 cup (250 ml) of syrup and transfer to clean saucepan. Bring to boil.

Add orange juice and rind; bring to boil again and continue cooking 3 minutes over high heat.

Mix cornstarch with 2 tbsp (30 ml) water; stir into orange syrup and cook 1 minute.

Mix in liqueur and pour sauce over pears. Cool before serving.

Buckwheat Crêpes with Peaches

(serves 6-8)

1 SERVING	264 CALORIES	32g CARBOHYDRATE
5g PROTEIN	13g FAT	1.1g FIBER

1 cup	(250 ml) buckwheat flour
¼ cup	(50 ml) all-purpose flour
½ tsp	(2 ml) salt
1½ cups	(375 ml) milk
3	beaten eggs
2 tbsp	(30 ml) melted butter
4 tbsp	(60 ml) butter
4 tbsp	(60 ml) brown sugar
5	large peaches, blanched, peeled and sliced
3 tbsp	(45 ml) rum
	icing sugar

Stir both flours and salt together in large bowl. Mix in milk until well incorporated, then add eggs; mix vigorously with whisk. Pass through sieve.

Stir in melted butter and refrigerate batter 1 hour.

Lightly butter crêpe pan and place over medium-high heat. Whisk batter well.

As butter melts, wipe off excess with paper towel. When pan is hot, pour in small ladle of batter and rotate pan to completely coat bottom.

Replace pan over heat and cook crêpe 1 minute until lightly browned.

Turn crêpe over (use long spatula rather than flipping) and continue cooking 1 minute.

Repeat for rest of batter, stacking cooked crêpes on large plate. During cooking wipe pan with butter as needed and monitor heat to keep it at medium-high.

For crêpe filling, heat 4 tbsp (60 ml) butter in saucepan. Add brown sugar and peaches; cook 2 minutes over medium-high heat.

Mix in rum and spoon peaches on middle of flat crêpes (keep some peaches for garnish). Fold crêpes into 4 and place on ovenproof platter.

Sprinkle with icing sugar and broil several minutes.

Serve with remaining peach slices.

Delicious Fruit Trifle

(serves 10-12)

1 SERVING	305 CALORIES	43g CARBOHYDRATE
5g PROTEIN	11g FAT	2.1g FIBER

4	egg yolks
½ cup	(125 ml) sugar
1 cup	(250 ml) boiled milk, tepid
1 tbsp	(15 ml) dark rum
1 cup	(250 ml) mixed berries
2 cups	(500 ml) blueberries
2 cups	(500 ml) diced watermelon
1	small angel or sponge cake, sliced into 3 layers
⅓ cup	(75 ml) light rum
3 cups	(750 ml) strawberries, hulled and halved
2½ cups	(625 ml) whipped cream

Place egg yolks and sugar in stainless steel bowl; beat together with electric beater until mixture forms ribbons.

Mix in milk until well incorporated. Stir in dark rum and set bowl over saucepan half-filled with hot water. Cook over medium heat while stirring constantly with wooden spoon. Do not boil.

When cream coats the back of the spoon, remove bowl from saucepan and set aside to cool.

Toss mixed berries, blueberries and watermelon together in small bowl.

When custard cream has cooled, begin building trifle in large glass bowl or substitute. Set one layer of cake in bottom followed by sprinkling of rum.

Continue with layer of strawberries, whipped cream, custard cream and mixed fruit.

Repeat layers until ingredients are used, ending with a generous topping of whipped cream.

If desired decorate trifle with glaze.

Fruit in the Shell

(serves 2)

1 SERVING	390 CALORIES	79g CARBOHYDRATE
2g PROTEIN	7g FAT	8.5g FIBER

1	small pear, peeled and diced
1	nectarine, diced
1	slice watermelon, seeded and diced
12	strawberries, hulled and halved
1	kiwi fruit, peeled and sliced
6-8	blackberries
¼ cup	(50 ml) blueberries
1 tbsp	(15 ml) soft butter
2 tbsp	(30 ml) sugar
3 tbsp	(45 ml) rum
1	pineapple
	juice 1 orange
	juice 1 lemon
	several pitted cherries
	few whole strawberries for decoration

Place pear, nectarine, watermelon, halved strawberries, kiwi fruit, blackberries and blueberries in mixing bowl; set aside.

Heat butter in frying pan over medium heat. Add sugar and cook 3 minutes over high heat while stirring constantly — mixture should become golden in color.

Add orange and lemon juices; mix well. Stir in rum and cook 3 minutes.

Pour syrup over fruit in bowl, toss and marinate 30 minutes.

Slice pineapple in half, lengthwise. Using sharp knife and spoon, cut and scoop out insides from shells. Reserve pineapple flesh for other recipes.

When fruit is ready, spoon into hollowed shells and decorate with cherries and whole strawberries.

Berries and Broiled Cream

(serves 4)

1 SERVING	355 CALORIES	39g CARBOHYDRATE
1g PROTEIN	22g FAT	2.4g FIBER

1 cup	(250 ml) strawberries, hulled and halved
1 cup	(250 ml) raspberries
2	kiwi fruit, peeled and sliced
1 cup	(250 ml) heavy cream, whipped
½ cup	(125 ml) brown sugar
½ cup	(125 ml) hot rum

Divide fruit among 4 individual baking dishes.

Top fruit with whipped cream and sprinkle with brown sugar. Broil for 1 minute in oven.

Remove from oven, sprinkle with rum and flambé.

Fruit à la Mode

(serves 4)

1 SERVING	398 CALORIES	63g CARBOHYDRATE
4g PROTEIN	13g FAT	4.2g FIBER

¼ cup	(50 ml) sugar
1 tsp	(5 ml) vanilla
1 cup	(250 ml) water
4	large peaches, blanched, peeled and halved
1 cup	(250 ml) strawberries, hulled and halved
1 cup	(250 ml) raspberries
2 tbsp	(30 ml) fine sugar
2 tbsp	(30 ml) Cointreau
4	large scoops vanilla ice cream
	whipped cream

Place sugar, vanilla and water in saucepan; bring to boil. Continue cooking 2 to 3 minutes over medium heat.

Add peaches and cook 2 minutes over medium heat. Remove pan from heat and let fruit cool in syrup.

Purée strawberries and raspberries in food processor. Transfer to nonstick frying pan and stir in fine sugar. Cook 3 minutes over medium heat.

Add liqueur and cook 1 more minute over high heat. Force mixture through sieve into bowl.

Spoon a bit of berry sauce into bottom of glass dessert dishes. Add a half peach and follow with scoop of ice cream.

Cover with another peach half, top with berry sauce and decorate with whipped cream.

Cheese Fruitcup

(serves 4)

1 SERVING	348 CALORIES	31g CARBOHYDRATE
5g PROTEIN	23g FAT	2.1g FIBER

2	kiwis, peeled and diced
2	bananas, peeled and sliced
1	apple, cored, peeled and sliced
4 tbsp	(60 ml) yogurt, flavor of your choice
2 tbsp	(30 ml) your preferred liqueur
8 oz	(250 g) package cream cheese, softened
	juice 1 orange

Place kiwis and bananas in food processor and purée.

Add apple and orange juice; continue blending several seconds.

Add yogurt, liqueur and cream cheese; blend well until quite smooth.

Spoon into small cup-like glasses and refrigerate before serving.

Blueberries in Syrup

(serves 4)

1 SERVING	295 CALORIES	46g CARBOHYDRATE
5g PROTEIN	10g FAT	2.1g FIBER

4 tbsp	(60 ml) brown sugar
1 tsp	(5 ml) vanilla
1 tbsp	(15 ml) grated lemon rind
1 tbsp	(15 ml) grated orange rind
1 cup	(250 ml) water
2 cups	(500 ml) blueberries
4	large scoops ice cream

Place sugar, vanilla, fruit rinds and water in saucepan; mix well and bring to boil. Cook 2 to 3 minutes over low heat until syrup thickens.

Stir in blueberries, remove saucepan from heat and let fruit cool in syrup.

Spoon blueberries over ice cream and serve.

Wally's Watermelon Punch

(serves 10-12)

1 SERVING	129 CALORIES	21g CARBOHYDRATE
0g PROTEIN	0g FAT	0.5g FIBER

½	watermelon, seeded and cubed
½ cup	(125 ml) lime juice
1 cup	(250 ml) light rum
4 cups	(1 L) orange juice
1 cup	(250 ml) pineapple juice
½ cup	(125 ml) fine sugar
	plenty of ice

Purée watermelon in food processor. Pass through sieve into large punch bowl.

Add remaining ingredients, mix very well and refrigerate 3 to 4 hours.

If desired, decorate with slices of fruit and serve in a bowl with plenty of ice.

Watermelon Compote

(serves 4)

1 SERVING	129 CALORIES	31g CARBOHYDRATE
1g PROTEIN	0g FAT	1.5g FIBER

¼ cup	(50 ml) brown sugar
½ cup	(125 ml) water
1 tbsp	(15 ml) grated lemon rind
2 cups	(500 ml) diced watermelon
2	large peaches, blanched, peeled and thinly sliced
½ cup	(125 ml) seedless green grapes
	juice 2 limes

Place sugar, water, lemon rind and lime juice in small saucepan. Bring to boil.

Add fruit and mix well; cover and cook 3 to 4 minutes over low heat.

Remove pan from heat and let fruit cool in syrup. Serve over ice cream.

Cantaloupe Tarts *(serves 4)*

1 SERVING	605 CALORIES	71g CARBOHYDRATE
9g PROTEIN	32g FAT	1.4g FIBER

1 cup	(250 ml) milk
1 tbsp	(15 ml) water
1 tsp	(5 ml) Pernod
½ cup	(125 ml) sugar
3	egg yolks
¼ cup	(50 ml) all-purpose flour, sifted
1	small ripe cantaloupe
8	cooked pastry tarts
	green maraschino cherries

Pour milk and water into medium-size saucepan. Bring to boil over medium heat. Stir in Pernod, remove from heat and set aside.

Place sugar and egg yolks in stainless steel bowl. Beat together with electric beater for 3 to 4 minutes or until eggs become foamy and almost white in color.

Mix in flour with whisk until well incorporated.

Gradually pour half of hot milk into bowl containing egg mixture, stirring constantly with whisk. Incorporate well.

Incorporate remaining milk and immediately place bowl over saucepan half-filled with hot water.

Cook over medium heat while whisking constantly until very thick and cream coats the back of a spoon.

Pour cream into clean bowl and let cool. Cover with buttered waxed paper and chill before using.

To prepare tarts, remove all seeds from cantaloupe. Slice into quarters and thinly slice flesh on slight angle.

Spread pastry cream in bottom of cooked tarts and arrange cantaloupe slices decoratively on top.

Serve tarts immediately or glaze if desired. Decorate with green maraschino cherries.

Banana Mousse

(serves 4)

1 SERVING	369 CALORIES	39g CARBOHYDRATE
4g PROTEIN	22g FAT	2.4g FIBER

¼ cup	(50 ml) sugar
⅓ cup	(75 ml) water
4	ripe bananas, peeled and sliced
¼ tsp	(1 ml) cinnamon
3	egg whites, beaten stiff
1 cup	(250 ml) heavy cream, whipped

Cook sugar and water together in saucepan 1 minute over medium heat.

Add bananas and cinnamon; cook 3 minutes over medium-high heat.

Transfer bananas to food processor and blend until puréed. Chill.

Transfer puréed bananas to mixing bowl. Fold in stiff egg whites until well incorporated.

Have whipped cream ready in large bowl. Fold banana mixture into cream using spatula until well incorporated.

Spoon into dessert dishes and chill before serving.

Macaroon Bananas

(serves 4)

1 SERVING	574 CALORIES	73g CARBOHYDRATE
8g PROTEIN	28g FAT	4.9g FIBER

4	large bananas
¼ cup	(50 ml) bourbon
1 tsp	(5 ml) lime juice
2	beaten eggs
1½ cups	(375 ml) crushed macaroons
3 tbsp	(45 ml) butter

Peel bananas and place them on large platter. Add bourbon and lime juice; marinate 1 hour.

Dip bananas in beaten eggs and roll in crushed macaroons.

Heat butter in large frying pan. Add bananas and cook 2 to 3 minutes over medium heat, turning to brown all sides.

If desired, flambé with heated marinade before serving.

Banana Flip

(serves 4)

1 SERVING	224 CALORIES	25g CARBOHYDRATE
4g PROTEIN	12g FAT	1.2g FIBER

2	bananas, peeled
1½ cups	(375 ml) cold milk
1 cup	(250 ml) cold light cream
2 tbsp	(30 ml) maple syrup
¼ cup	(50 ml) dark rum
	few drops lime juice
	orange slices for decoration

Place bananas in blender and purée.

Add milk, cream, maple syrup, rum and lime juice; continue blending until well mixed and frothy.

Pour into tall-stemmed glasses and decorate with orange slices.

Passion Fruit Cream Dessert

(serves 4)

1 SERVING	333 CALORIES	49g CARBOHYDRATE
7g PROTEIN	12g FAT	—g FIBER

4	egg yolks
½ cup	(125 ml) sugar
1 cup	(250 ml) boiled milk, tepid
1 tbsp	(15 ml) rum
4	passion fruits
3 tbsp	(45 ml) heavy cream

Place egg yolks and sugar in stainless steel bowl; beat together with electric beater until mixture forms ribbons.

Mix in milk until well incorporated. Stir in rum and set bowl over saucepan half-filled with hot water. Cook over medium heat while stirring constantly with wooden spoon. Do not boil.

When cream coats the back of the spoon, remove bowl from saucepan and set aside to cool.

Slice passion fruits in half, widthwise. Using spoon, scoop out pulp and seeds and place in blender. Add heavy cream and blend at medium speed for 1 minute.

Pour blended fruit into custard cream and mix. Serve cold in dessert bowls.

Mango Sherbet

1 SERVING	174 CALORIES	40g CARBOHYDRATE
0g PROTEIN	0g FAT	0.9g FIBER

3½ lb	(1.6 kg) ripe mangoes
1 cup	(250 ml) granulated sugar
⅔ cup	(150 ml) water
3 tbsp	(45 ml) white rum
	juice 3 limes

Peel mangoes and slice off flesh from pits. Purée fruit in food processor and transfer to bowl.

Place sugar and water in small saucepan; cook 5 minutes over high heat.

Remove saucepan from heat and let syrup cool.

Add syrup, rum and lime juice to mangoes in bowl; mix well.

Freeze following the directions for your particular brand of ice cream maker.

Mango Salad

(serves 4)

1 SERVING	176 CALORIES	31g CARBOHYDRATE
8g PROTEIN	2g FAT	0.9g FIBER

2	large mangoes
3 tbsp	(45 ml) fine sugar
1-1½ cups	(250-375 ml) cottage cheese
1½ cups	(375 ml) raspberries
	juice 2 limes

Using sharp knife, run blade around mangoes against the large flat pit. Peel one half and slice flesh in wedges. Repeat for other side.

Place all wedges in bowl; add lime juice and sugar. Marinate 30 minutes.

Scoop cottage cheese onto dessert plates or in bowls. Surround with mangoes and top with raspberries. Serve.

Mango Mousse

(serves 4)

1 SERVING	260 CALORIES	35g CARBOHYDRATE
3g PROTEIN	12g FAT	1.4g FIBER

3	mangoes, peeled and sliced
3 cups	(750 ml) water
¼ cup	(50 ml) sugar
½ cup	(125 ml) heavy cream, whipped
3	egg whites, beaten stiff
	juice ½ lemon
	chocolate shavings

Place sliced mangoes in saucepan. Add water, sugar and lemon juice; cook 5 to 6 minutes over medium heat.

Force mixture through sieve into bowl; set aside to cool.

Incorporate whipped cream, then fold in beaten egg whites until well incorporated.

Chill before serving and decorate with chocolate shavings.

Mango and Prosciutto

(serves 4)

1 SERVING	138 CALORIES	23g CARBOHYDRATE
7g PROTEIN	2g FAT	1.4g FIBER

3	mangoes, peeled
¼ lb	(125 g) prosciutto slices
	lime slices
	ground pepper

Slice mangoes into 1 inch (2.5 cm) pieces.

Cut prosciutto slices into 3 and wrap around mango pieces; secure with toothpicks.

Serve with lime slices and season well with pepper.

Raspberry Rice Pudding

(serves 4-6)

1 SERVING	355 CALORIES	72g CARBOHYDRATE
7g PROTEIN	4g FAT	1.7g FIBER

2½ cups	(625 ml) salted water
1 cup	(250 ml) long grain rice, rinsed
3 cups	(750 ml) milk
1 cup	(250 ml) sugar
1 tsp	(5 ml) vanilla
½ tsp	(2 ml) nutmeg
1½ cups	(375 ml) raspberries

Pour salted water into saucepan and bring to boil. Mix in rice, cover and cook 19 to 21 minutes over low heat.

Add milk, half of sugar, vanilla and nutmeg; bring to boil. Mix rice well and cover saucepan; cook 30 to 35 minutes over low heat. Stir 2 to 3 times.

Transfer cooked rice to 8 cup (2 L) soufflé mold; refrigerate to cool.

Meanwhile, place raspberries and remaining sugar in small saucepan. Partially cover and cook 4 to 5 minutes.

Purée in food processor and spread over rice pudding. Serve.

Chestnut Parfait

(serves 4)

1 SERVING	395 CALORIES	47g CARBOHYDRATE
7g PROTEIN	20g FAT	0.8g FIBER

⅓ cup	(75 ml) granulated sugar
4	egg yolks
2 tbsp	(30 ml) rum
1 cup	(250 ml) hot milk
¼ cup	(50 ml) candied fruit
1 cup	(250 ml) canned puréed chestnuts
2 cups	(500 ml) whipped cream

Place sugar, egg yolks and rum in bowl. Mix together with electric beater until fluffy — about 2 minutes.

Pour in hot milk and whisk well. Cook cream in double-boiler until it coats the back of a spoon. Whisk constantly!

Stir in candied fruit.

Choose tall dessert glasses and spoon layer of puréed chestnuts in bottom. Follow with layer of custard cream and repeat until ingredients are used.

Top parfaits with whipped cream and if desired decorate with icing.

Place sugar, egg yolks and rum in bowl.

Mix together with electric beater until fluffy — about 2 minutes.

Pour in hot milk and whisk well.

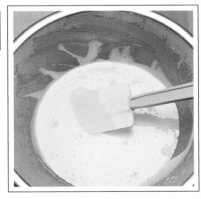

After cream has cooked, begin layering the puréed chestnuts and custard cream in tall dessert glasses.

Place flour,  ¾ cup (175 ml) butter and cinnamon in bowl.

1

Add granulated sugar.

2

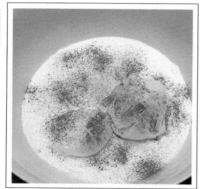

Add 2 eggs and vanilla.

3

Incorporate with pastry blender.

4

Apple Galette

(serves 6-8)

1 SERVING	536 CALORIES	77g CARBOHYDRATE
5g PROTEIN	23g FAT	1.8g FIBER

2 cups	(500 ml) all-purpose flour
¾ cup	(175 ml) softened butter
1 tsp	(5 ml) cinnamon
¾ cup	(175 ml) granulated sugar
2	eggs
1 tsp	(5 ml) vanilla
2 tbsp	(30 ml) cold water
2 tbsp	(30 ml) butter
4	apples, cored, peeled and sliced
⅓ cup	(75 ml) brown sugar
1 tbsp	(15 ml) grated lemon rind
1 cup	(250 ml) icing sugar
2 tbsp	(30 ml) lemon juice
1 tbsp	(15 ml) hot water
	beaten egg

Place flour, ¾ cup (175 ml) butter and cinnamon in bowl. Add granulated sugar, 2 eggs and vanilla; incorporate with pastry blender.

Add cold water and pinch dough to incorporate. Shape into ball and cover with waxed paper; refrigerate 2 hours.

Preheat oven to 350°F (180°C).

When ready to prepare galette, cut dough in half. Roll both on floured surface until about ¼ inch (0.65 cm) thick. Dust with more flour if needed. Place 9 inch (23 cm) plate on dough and trace galettes. Cut away excess dough to form circles.

Place galettes on separate buttered and floured cookie sheets; brush lightly with beaten egg. Bake 10 minutes.

Set aside to cool while you prepare the filling.

Melt 2 tbsp (30 ml) butter in frying pan. Add apples and cook 15 minutes over high heat, stirring frequently.

Sprinkle in brown sugar and lemon rind; continue cooking 3 minutes.

Remove frying pan from heat and set aside to cool.

Meanwhile, prepare icing by placing icing sugar, lemon juice and hot water in small bowl. Mix together.

To assemble dessert, place one galette on bottom of serving platter. Cover with cooled apples and top with second galette. Generously spread lemon icing over top, letting it drip down sides. Decorate with additional colored icings if desired.

Slice (carefully) and serve.

Rhubarb and Raspberry Compote

(serves 4)

1 SERVING	319 CALORIES	64g CARBOHYDRATE
2g PROTEIN	6g FAT	5.3g FIBER

1 cup	(250 ml) sugar
1¼ cups	(300 ml) water
1½ lb	(750 g) diced rhubarb
1¼ cups	(300 ml) raspberries
3 tbsp	(45 ml) grated orange rind
	juice 1 lime
	heavy cream

Place sugar and water in large saucepan. Cook 4 to 5 minutes over medium-low heat or until sugar is melted.

Stir in rhubarb and lime juice; cook 10 minutes over low heat.

Add raspberries and orange rind; mix well. Continue cooking 3 minutes.

Spoon compote into dessert bowls and serve with heavy cream.

Super-Moist Cheesecake

(serves 10-12)

| 1 SERVING | 410 CALORIES | 32g CARBOHYDRATE |
| 6g PROTEIN | 29g FAT | 0.1g FIBER |

2	8 oz (250 g) packages cream cheese, softened
½ cup	(125 ml) granulated sugar
3 tbsp	(45 ml) Tia Maria liqueur
2 tbsp	(30 ml) cornstarch
4	egg yolks
1 cup	(250 ml) heavy cream, whipped
4	egg whites, beaten stiff
14 oz	(398 ml) can pitted Bing cherries
¼ cup	(50 ml) granulated sugar
1 tbsp	(15 ml) cornstarch
3 tbsp	(45 ml) cold water
	graham crumb bottom crust, cooked in 10 inch (25 cm) spring-form cake pan

Preheat oven to 300°F (150°C).

Place cheese and ½ cup (125 ml) sugar in bowl of electric mixer. Mix at medium speed until creamed.

Add liqueur and 2 tbsp (30 ml) cornstarch; continue mixing until completely incorporated and smooth.

Add egg yolks and mix very well — about 2 minutes.

Add whipped cream and continue mixing until incorporated.

Remove bowl from mixer and fold in beaten egg whites with spatula. Continue folding until well incorporated.

Pour batter into cake pan prepared with crumb crust and bake 1¼-1½ hours or until toothpick inserted comes out clean.

Remove cake from oven and let cool in pan.

Unmold and refrigerate 1 hour.

Meanwhile, begin preparing topping. Pour cherry juice (set cherries aside) and ¼ cup (50 ml) sugar in small saucepan. Bring to boil and continue cooking 2-3 minutes.

Mix 1 tbsp (15 ml) cornstarch with 3 tbsp (45 ml) cold water; stir into sauce and continue cooking 1 minute over medium heat.

When sauce has thickened enough, stir in cherries and set aside on counter to cool.

Spread cherries over cheesecake, slice and serve.

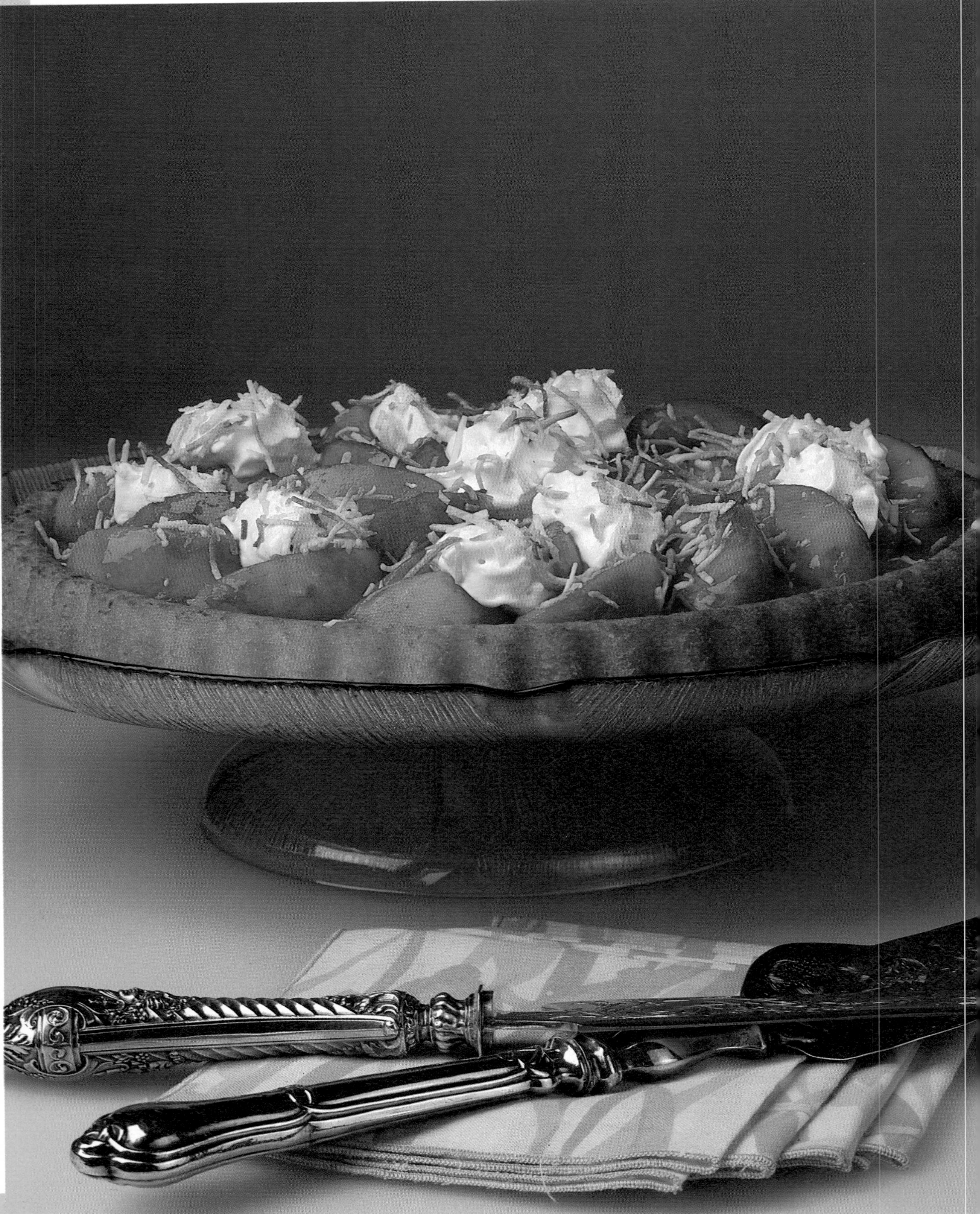

One Layer Fruit Cake

(serves 4-8)

1 SERVING	262 CALORIES	51g CARBOHYDRATE
3g PROTEIN	5g FAT	0.9g FIBER

4	ripe nectarines
2	ripe peaches
½ cup	(125 ml) sugar
1 cup	(250 ml) water
1	1.2 oz (34 g) package glaze mix, prepared
1	6 oz (169 g) short-cake layer
	juice 1 orange
	whipped cream for decoration

Cut fruit in half to remove pits — if they are not ripe this might be difficult.

Cut halves into quarters and set aside.

Place sugar, water and orange juice in saucepan; bring to boil. Continue cooking 3 to 4 minutes over high heat.

Add fruit to hot liquid in saucepan and bring to boiling point. Reduce heat to medium-low and continue cooking 2 minutes.

Remove fruit from liquid, peel and cut quarters in half; set aside on plate.

Replace saucepan containing syrup over heat and bring to boil.

Remove from heat and mix ⅓ cup (75 ml) of syrup into prepared glaze mix. Generously spread glaze over bottom of cake.

Arrange fruit on cake over glaze and brush with any remaining glaze.

Refrigerate before serving. Decorate with whipped cream and if desired, sprinkle with coconut.

1 Cut fruit in half to remove pits — if they are not ripe this might be difficult.

3 Mix ⅓ cup (75 ml) of syrup into prepared glaze mix.

2 Add fruit to syrup mixture in saucepan and bring to boiling point. Reduce heat to medium-low and continue cooking 2 minutes.

4 Generously spread glaze over bottom of cake and arrange fruit on top. Brush with leftover glaze.

Afternoon Rum Cake

(serves 8-10)

1 SERVING	524 CALORIES	51g CARBOHYDRATE
9g PROTEIN	32g FAT	0.3g FIBER

1½ cups	(300 ml) softened butter
1 cup	(250 ml) granulated sugar
5	eggs
3 cups	(750 ml) all-purpose flour
1 tsp	(5 ml) cinnamon
2 tsp	(10 ml) baking powder
2 tbsp	(30 ml) dark rum
1 cup	(250 ml) milk
½ cup	(125 ml) slivered almonds
	grated rind 1 lemon
	pinch salt
	icing sugar

Preheat oven to 325°F (160°C). Generously butter 10 inch (25 cm) spring-form cake pan.

Place butter and lemon rind in large bowl; work butter until pliable.

Add sugar and cream together using spatula.

Add 1 egg and 3 tbsp (45 ml) flour and cinnamon; beat together with electric beater.

Add remaining eggs and beat until completely incorporated.

Place remaining flour with baking powder and salt in small bowl; mix together.

Sift half into egg batter and mix very well with spatula.

Pour in rum and incorporate with spatula.

Add remaining flour and continue incorporating.

Pour in milk and with spatula, mix until incorporated. Fold in almonds.

Pour batter into prepared cake pan and rap bottom against counter to settle mixture. Bake 40 minutes or until toothpick inserted comes out clean.

Remove pan from oven and cool 5-6 minutes.

Unmold onto wire rack and set aside until cold.

Place icing sugar in wire sieve and dust cake just before serving.

Place butter and lemon rind in bowl; work butter until pliable.

Add sugar and cream together using spatula.

Add 1 egg, 3 tbsp (45 ml) flour and cinnamon; beat together with electric beater.

After remaining eggs have been added, start adding the rest of the flour.

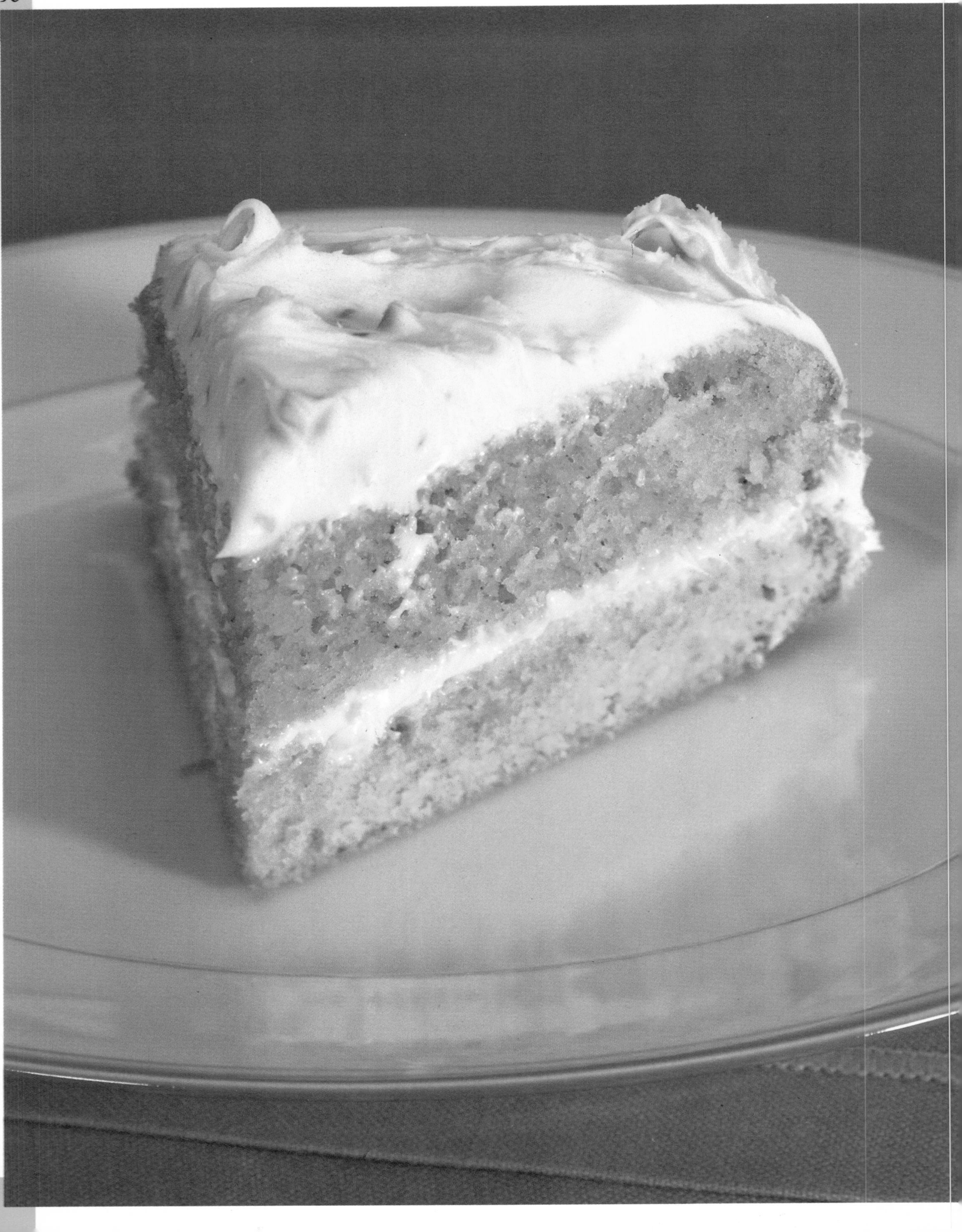

Midnight Snacking Cake

(serves 6-8)

1 SERVING	240 CALORIES	25g CARBOHYDRATE
4g PROTEIN	14g FAT	0g FIBER

½ cup	(125 ml) softened butter
½ cup	(125 ml) granulated sugar
1 tsp	(5 ml) cinnamon
3	eggs
4 tbsp	(60 ml) rum
1¼ cups	(300 ml) all-purpose flour
	pinch salt

Preheat oven to 350°F (180°C). Butter 10 inch (25 cm) spring-form cake pan.

Place butter, sugar and cinnamon in bowl; cream together.

Add first egg and beat well with electric beater.

Add remaining eggs, one at a time, beating well after each addition. Add rum during this time.

Mix flour with salt; stir into batter and mix with spatula until smooth.

Pour batter into prepared cake pan and bake 40-45 minutes or until toothpick inserted comes out clean.

Cool in pan about 10-15 minutes before unmolding cake onto wire rack for continued cooling.

Ice with vanilla icing or another one of your favorites.

1 Place butter, sugar and cinnamon in bowl; cream together.

2 Add eggs, one at a time, beating well after each addition. At some point during this time, add the rum too.

3 Mix flour with salt; stir into batter and mix with spatula until smooth.

4 Pour batter into prepared cake pan.

Raisin Almond Fruit Cake

(serves 8-10)

1 SERVING	619 CALORIES	59g CARBOHYDRATE
9g PROTEIN	39g FAT	2.1g FIBER

1¾ cups	(425 ml) all-purpose flour
1 tbsp	(15 ml) baking powder
¾ cup	(175 ml) sultana raisins
1 cup	(250 ml) chopped walnuts
1 cup	(250 ml) slivered almonds
1 cup	(250 ml) all-vegetable shortening
½ cup	(125 ml) brown sugar
½ cup	(125 ml) granulated sugar
4	eggs
½ cup	(125 ml) chopped candied mixed fruit
¼ cup	(50 ml) Tia Maria
	pinch salt
	pinch powdered ginger

Preheat oven to 325°F (160°C). Butter 8 inch (20 cm) square cake pan.

Sift flour, baking powder, salt and ginger into bowl.

Place raisins, walnuts and almonds in another bowl; add ⅓ of flour mixture. Toss and set aside.

Place shortening, brown and granulated sugar in bowl containing just flour. Incorporate well with pastry blender.

Add eggs and blend well with wooden spoon.

Incorporate raisin/flour mixture along with candied fruit; mix very well with wooden spoon.

Pour in Tia Maria and blend well. Pour batter into prepared cake pan and bake 1 hour or until toothpick inserted comes out clean.

Cool cake in pan before unmolding onto wire rack.

Serve with tea, coffee, as a snack or in your children's lunches as a nutritious dessert.

Sift flour, baking powder, salt and ginger into bowl.

Place shortening, brown and granulated sugar in bowl containing just flour. Incorporate well with pastry blender.

Place raisins, walnuts and almonds in another bowl; add ⅓ of flour mixture. Toss and set aside.

Add eggs and blend well with wooden spoon.

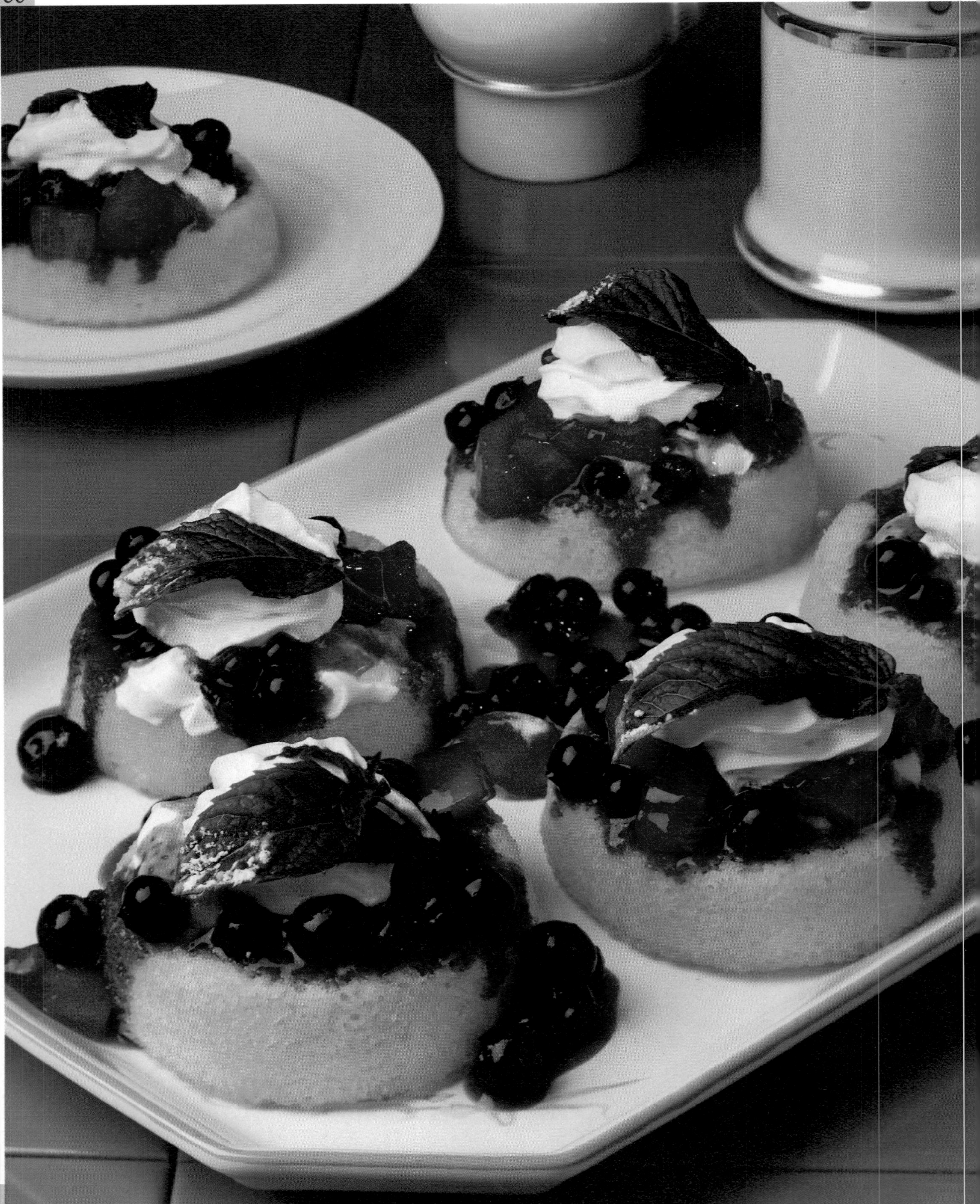

Blueberry and Papaya Cakes

(serves 6)

1 SERVING	233 CALORIES	43g CARBOHYDRATE
4g PROTEIN	5g FAT	1.3g FIBER

½	papaya
⅓ cup	(75 ml) sugar
¼ cup	(50 ml) water
1½ cups	(375 ml) blueberries
¼ cup	(50 ml) orange juice
2 tsp	(10 ml) cornstarch
3 tbsp	(45 ml) cold water
6	cake dessert shells
	dash grated lemon rind
	whipped cream to taste

Slice half papaya in half again, lengthwise. Seed, peel and dice flesh.

Place papaya in saucepan with sugar and ¼ cup (50 ml) water. Bring to boil over medium heat and continue cooking 3 minutes.

Stir in blueberries, orange juice and lemon rind; bring to boil again.

Mix cornstarch with 3 tbsp (45 ml) water; stir into cooking fruit and cook 1 more minute.

Pour into bowl and refrigerate until cold.

Fill cakes with whipped cream to taste; arrange on attractive serving platter.

Spoon fruit topping over cream, letting it drip down sides of cakes. Decorate with more whipped cream and serve.

Orange Cake Sauce

¼ cup (50 ml)	93 CALORIES	23g CARBOHYDRATE
0g PROTEIN	0g FAT	0.5g FIBER

1		small orange
1		lime
½		lemon
½ cup	(125 ml)	strawberries, hulled
½ cup	(125 ml)	brown sugar
½ cup	(125 ml)	granulated sugar
⅔ cup	(150 ml)	water
1 oz	(30 ml)	rum

Slice orange and lime in half; remove seeds and dice with rind. Dice ½ seeded lemon with rind as well.

Place diced fruit in food processor and mix well. Add strawberries and blend 30 seconds; set aside.

Place both sugars and water in saucepan; bring to boil. Continue cooking until temperature reaches 260°F (125°C). If you do not have a candy thermometer, drop a bit of syrup in cold water — if it forms a soft ball, it has reached the correct temperature.

Remove saucepan from stove, cool 5 minutes, then add fruit and rum.

Cool sauce before serving over cake.

Almond Brownies

(serves 6-8)

1 SERVING	410 CALORIES	33g CARBOHYDRATE
7g PROTEIN	28g FAT	0.7g FIBER

2 oz	(60 g) unsweetened chocolate
½ cup	(125 ml) softened butter
¾ cup	(175 ml) granulated sugar
3 tbsp	(45 ml) honey
1 tsp	(5 ml) vanilla
2	eggs
½ cup	(125 ml) sifted all-purpose flour
1 cup	(250 ml) slivered almonds
1	egg white, beaten stiff
	pinch salt

Preheat oven to 350°F (180°C). Butter 8 inch (20 cm) square cake pan.

Place chocolate in stainless steel bowl. Melt over saucepan half-filled with boiling water.

Place butter, sugar and honey in large bowl. Add melted chocolate and mix well.

Add vanilla and eggs, one at a time, beating well after each addition. It is best to use electric beater.

Fold in flour and salt and mix until completely incorporated. Stir in almonds and incorporate stiff egg white.

Pour batter into prepared cake pan and bake 25-30 minutes or until toothpick inserted comes out clean.

Cool brownies in pan 10-15 minutes, then finish cooling on wire rack. Serve with cold milk if desired.

Add melted chocolate to butter, sugar and honey placed in large bowl. Mix well. **1**

3 Fold in flour and salt and mix until completely incorporated.

Add vanilla and first egg; beat well before adding second egg. **2**

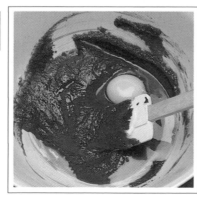

4 Stir in almonds and incorporate stiff egg white.

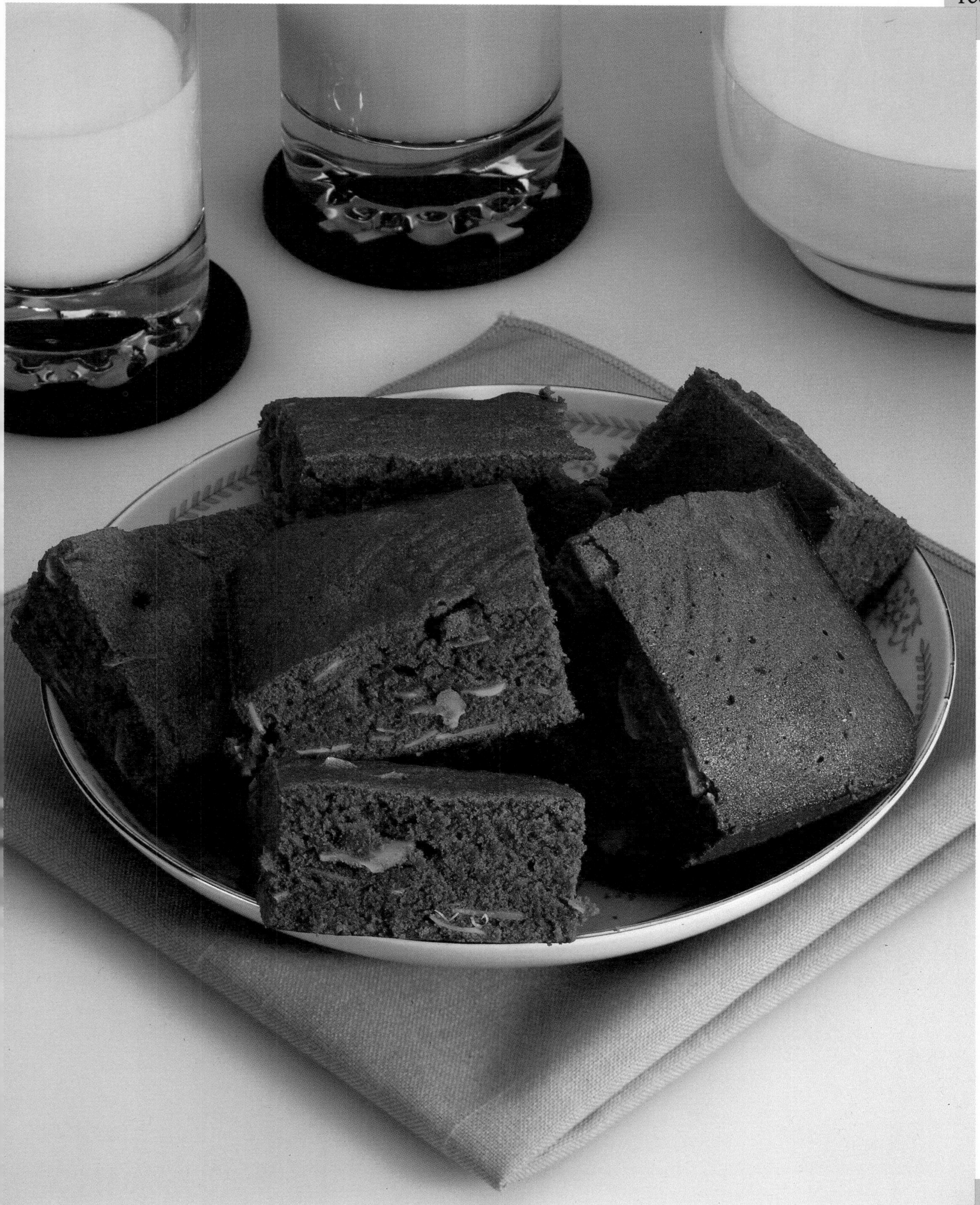

Papaya Pie

(serves 6-8)

1 SERVING	336 CALORIES	47g CARBOHYDRATE
3g PROTEIN	15g FAT	1.0g FIBER

4	large ripe papayas, peeled
¾ cup	(175 ml) granulated sugar
1 tsp	(5 ml) nutmeg
1 tsp	(5 ml) cinnamon
2 tbsp	(30 ml) butter
2 tbsp	(30 ml) cornstarch
1	beaten egg
	enough dough for bottom and top crusts*

Preheat oven to 425°F (220°C).

Cut papayas in half, seed and slice ½ inch (1.2 cm) thick. Place in bowl with sugar, nutmeg, cinnamon, butter and cornstarch; mix well.

Line 10 inch (25 cm) pie plate with half of rolled dough.

Add papaya filling and brush edges of dough with a bit of water.

Cover with top crust and pinch edges shut. Score top several times and brush with beaten egg.

Bake 7 minutes.

Reduce heat to 350°F (180°C) and continue baking 35-40 minutes. Note: If upper crust browns too quickly, cover with small sheet of aluminum foil.

Let cool slightly before serving.

* If desired you can use the dough recipe from the Blueberry Pie.

Cold Lime Soufflé

(serves 4-6)

1 SERVING	326 CALORIES	32g CARBOHYDRATE
7g PROTEIN	19g FAT	0g FIBER

2	small envelopes unflavored gelatine
¼ cup	(50 ml) cold water
4	egg yolks
¾ cup	(175 ml) super-fine sugar
4	egg whites, beaten stiff
1 cup	(250 ml) heavy cream, whipped
	juice of 6 large limes

Sprinkle gelatine over water poured into small bowl; set aside.

Place egg yolks and sugar in large bowl; mix together with whisk.

If bowl is stainless steel, set over saucepan half-filled with boiling water. Otherwise, use double-boiler.

Reduce heat to low and cook while whisking constantly until mixture becomes thick enough to coat the back of a spoon.

Whisk in gelatine and cook 1 more minute.

Squeeze in lime juice, whisk quickly and remove from heat.

Set aside to cool.

When egg yolks are cool, incorporate beaten egg whites by folding in with spatula.

Fold in whipped cream, incorporating with spatula.

Attach a foil collar around the outside edge of 4 cup (1 L) soufflé mold. Tape to secure.

Pour in soufflé mixture and refrigerate 4 hours.

Remove collar and serve with a fruit sauce if desired.

Lime Pie

(serves 6)

1 SERVING	443 CALORIES	48g CARBOHYDRATE
9g PROTEIN	24g FAT	0g FIBER

9 inch	(23 cm) pie shell
1¼ cups	(300 ml) can sweetened condensed milk
3	egg yolks
2 tbsp	(30 ml) grated lime rind
½ cup	(125 ml) lime juice
2	egg whites, beaten stiff
½ cup	(125 ml) heavy cream, whipped stiff

Bake pie shell in oven preheated at 425°F (220°C) for 12 to 15 minutes. Remove and set aside to cool.

Place milk, egg yolks, lime rind and juice in stainless steel bowl. Set over saucepan half-filled with hot water on medium-low heat. Cook mixture until thickened, stirring constantly.

Transfer bowl to counter and let cool.

Fold in egg whites, then whipped cream, with spatula.

Pour filling into pie shell and refrigerate overnight. Garnish pie with roasted almonds or with slices of lime if desired.

Blueberry Pie

(serves 6-8)

1 SERVING	433 CALORIES	65g CARBOHYDRATE
3g PROTEIN	18g FAT	2.1g FIBER

2 cups	(500 ml) all-purpose flour
⅔ cup	(150 ml) all-vegetable shortening
5-6 tbsp	(75-90 ml) cold water
1¼ cups	(300 ml) granulated sugar
3 tbsp	(45 ml) cornstarch
4 cups	(1 L) thawed blueberries
1 tbsp	(15 ml) melted butter
1 tbsp	(15 ml) grated lemon rind
	several pinches salt
	light cream

Sift flour with one pinch salt into large bowl. Add shortening and incorporate with pastry blender.

Knead in enough cold water to form a ball. Wrap in waxed paper and refrigerate 2-3 hours.

Preheat oven to 425°F (220°C).

Cut dough in half. Roll out on floured surface and line 10 inch (25 cm) pie plate. Set aside.

Place sugar, cornstarch and remaining ingredients in saucepan; mix well. Cook 15 minutes over low heat.

Pour cooled berry mixture into pie shell. Cover with top crust and pinch edges shut. Score top several times and brush with light cream.

Bake 10 minutes.

Reduce heat to 375°F (190°C) and continue baking 45 minutes.

Let cool slightly before serving.

Sift flour and salt into large bowl.

Add shortening and incorporate with pastry blender — the dough will begin to take shape.

Add water as required and knead dough to form ball. The dough should be pliable and all ingredients completely combined.

Wrap dough in waxed paper and refrigerate 2-3 hours.

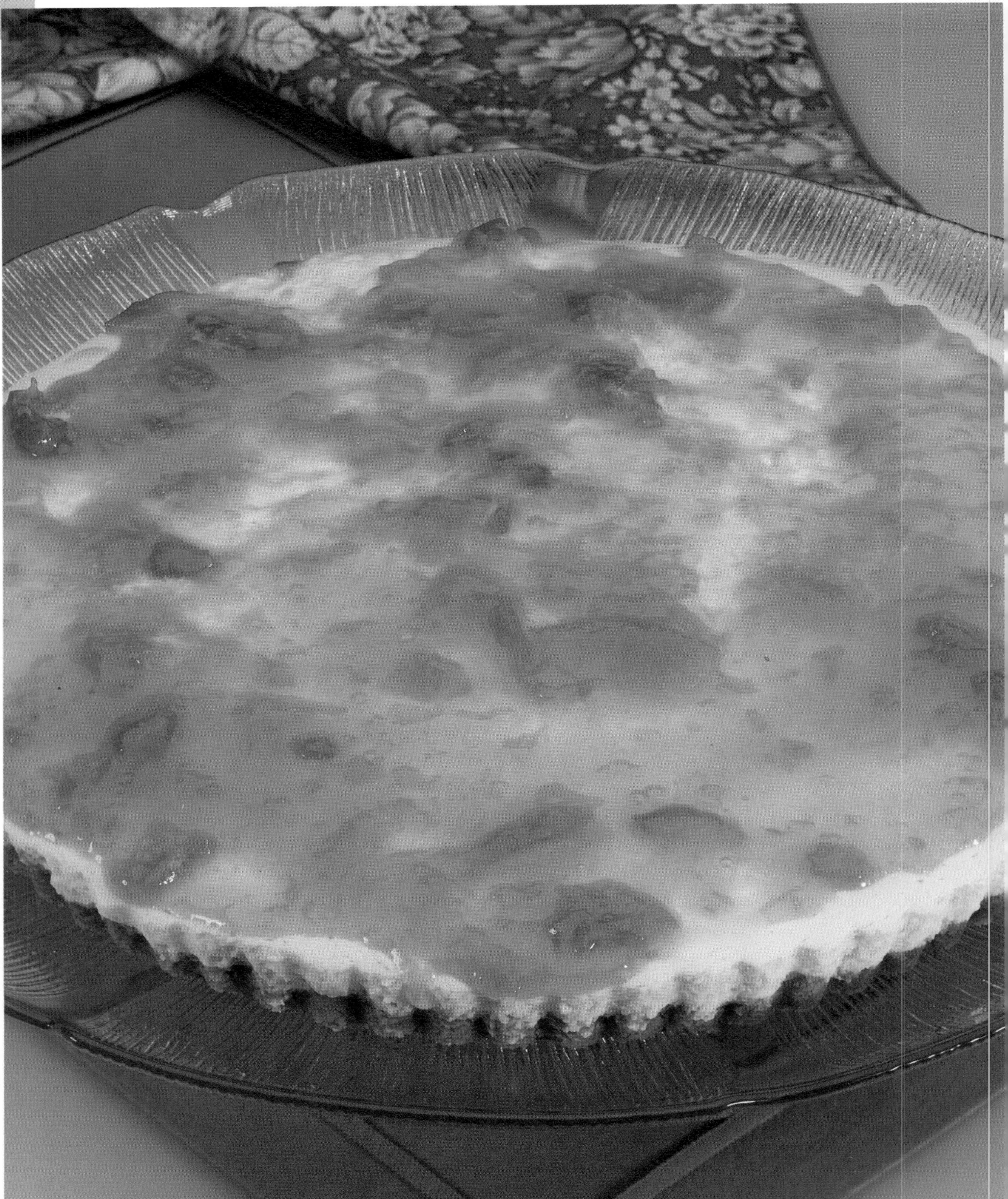

Rum Graham Pie

(serves 6-8)

1 SERVING	419 CALORIES	43g CARBOHYDRATE
7g PROTEIN	23g FAT	0.5g FIBER

1½ cups	(375 ml) graham crumbs
½ cup	(125 ml) brown sugar
¼ cup	(50 ml) softened butter
¼ cup	(50 ml) cold water
1	small envelope unflavored gelatine
3	egg yolks
¼ cup	(50 ml) granulated sugar
¼ cup	(50 ml) rum
¼ cup	(50 ml) light cream
3	egg whites, beaten stiff
1 cup	(250 ml) heavy cream, whipped
	grated rind 1 orange

Preheat oven to 375°F (190°C).

Place graham crumbs and half of brown sugar in bowl; mix together.

Add butter and incorporate well. Press mixture into 10 inch (25 cm) spring-form cake pan. Bake 8 minutes. Remove from oven and set aside.

Pour cold water into small bowl. Sprinkle in gelatine and let stand without stirring.

Place egg yolks in large bowl. Add remaining brown sugar and all of granulated sugar; beat well with electric beater.

Mix in orange rind. Pour in rum and light cream; mix well.

Cook pastry cream in double-boiler until it coats the back of a spoon. Whisk constantly!

Incorporate gelatine and whisk 30 seconds. Remove from heat and refrigerate.

When custard cream is cold and almost settled, incorporate egg whites and whipped cream with whisk.

Make a collar from double sheets of foil that can be placed around the cake pan to help keep the cream mixture in position during chilling. Tape securely to pan.

Once the collar is positioned correctly, pour in the rum cream mixture and refrigerate overnight.

Unmold. Serve plain or with a variety of fruit toppings.

Place egg yolks in large bowl with remaining brown sugar and all of granulated sugar; beat well.

Be sure to beat the egg whites until stiff. Notice how they form peaks.

Mix in orange rind. Pour in rum and light cream; mix well.

When custard cream is cold and almost settled, incorporate egg whites and whipped cream.

Rhubarb Pie

(serves 6)

1 SERVING	476 CALORIES	71g CARBOHYDRATE
5g PROTEIN	19g FAT	2.4g FIBER

1½ lb	(750 g) cubed rhubarb
¾ cup	(175 ml) granulated sugar
¾ cup	(175 ml) brown sugar
2 tbsp	(30 ml) grated lemon rind
2½ tbsp	(40 ml) cornstarch
2	large eggs
2 tbsp	(30 ml) heavy cream
	pastry dough for pie shell and top crust

Preheat oven to 425°F (220°C).

Mix rhubarb with sugars, lemon rind and cornstarch; toss to evenly coat.

Beat eggs with cream; pour half over rhubarb and mix.

Spoon rhubarb into uncooked pie shell. Cover with top crust, crimp edges and prick with fork or knife. Brush with remaining beaten eggs.

Bake 25 minutes in oven.

Reduce heat to 350°F (180°C) and continue baking 15 minutes.

Cool before serving.

Rum Cream Pie

(serves 6-8)

1 SERVING	260 CALORIES	23g CARBOHYDRATE
2g PROTEIN	16g FAT	0g FIBER

3	egg yolks
½ cup	(125 ml) granulated sugar
1 tbsp	(15 ml) grated lemon rind
1 cup	(250 ml) hot milk
4 tbsp	(60 ml) rum
1	small envelope unflavored gelatine
½ cup	(125 ml) heavy cream, whipped
3	egg whites, beaten stiff
9 inch	(23 cm) pie shell, precooked
	grated sweet chocolate

Place egg yolks and sugar in large bowl and mix with electric beater until color changes to nearly white.

Stir in lemon rind. Pour in hot milk and whisk very well.

Pour rum into small bowl and sprinkle in gelatine; set aside.

Cook milk mixture in double-boiler until cream coats the back of a spoon. It is essential to whisk constantly.

Add gelatine and continue cooking 1 more minute, whisking constantly.

Refrigerate cream until it settles and starts to cling to the sides of the bowl.

Remove cream from refrigerator and fold in whipped cream. Incorporate with whisk.

Fold in beaten egg whites and gently whisk to finish incorporating. Refrigerate 5-6 minutes.

Whisk mixture again and pour into prepared pie shell. Refrigerate 6 hours.

Dust with grated chocolate just before serving.

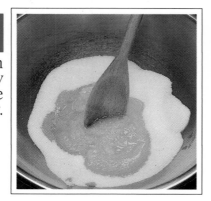

Place egg **1** yolks and sugar in large bowl, preferably stainless steel for use later as double-boiler.

3 Pour in hot milk and whisk very well.

Mix with **2** electric beater until color changes to nearly white. Stir in lemon rind.

4 After cream has been cooked and chilled, fold in whipped cream and incorporate with whisk.

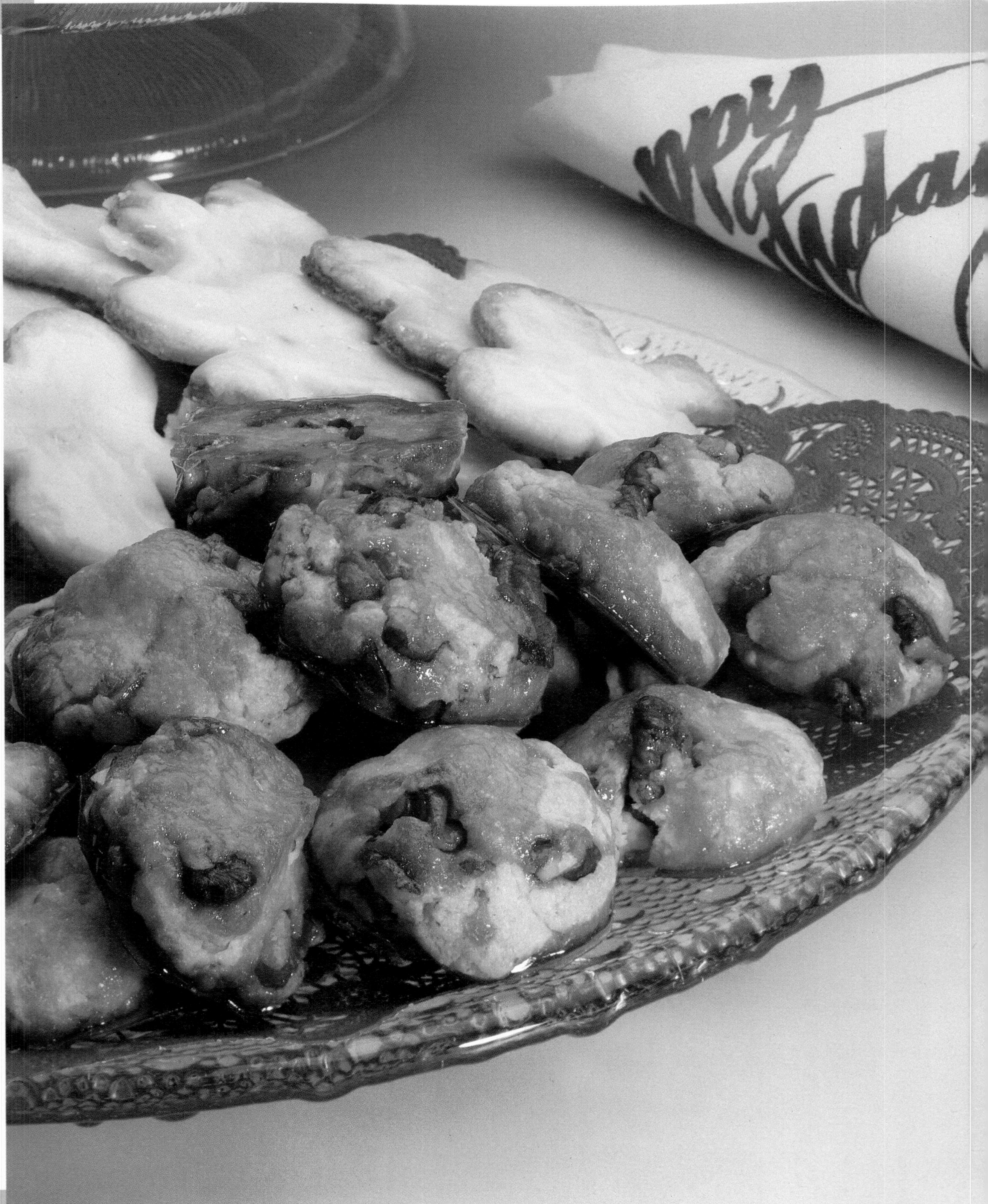

Honey Walnut Clusters

(yield: 24-36)

2 CLUSTERS	140 CALORIES	13g CARBOHYDRATE
2g PROTEIN	9g FAT	0.2g FIBER

⅓ cup	(75 ml) granulated sugar
½ cup	(125 ml) softened butter
1 tsp	(5 ml) vanilla
1¼ cups	(300 ml) all-purpose flour
¾ cup	(175 ml) chopped walnuts
¼ cup	(50 ml) light cream
¼ cup	(50 ml) liquid honey

Prepare cookie sheet by lining it with sheet of lightly buttered aluminum foil; set aside.

Place sugar and butter in large bowl; cream together.

Add vanilla and flour; combine with pastry blender.

Mix in walnuts. Add cream and blend everything together (best to use your hands) until well incorporated.

Knead with heel of your hand and shape into ball. Cover with waxed paper and refrigerate 30 minutes.

Preheat oven to 350°F (180°C).

Drop about 1 tbsp (15 ml) of cookie dough onto prepared sheet. Flatten slightly with fork, brush tops with honey and bake 18-20 minutes.

Cool cookies on wire racks.

Place sugar and butter in large bowl; cream together.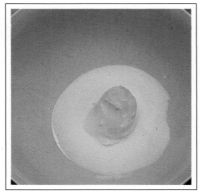

Mix in walnuts. Add cream and blend everything together.

Add vanilla and flour; combine with pastry blender.

Knead dough with the heel of your hand and shape into ball for chilling.

Lemon Glazed Cookies

(yield: 24-36)

2 COOKIES	145 CALORIES	16g CARBOHYDRATE
0g PROTEIN	9g FAT	0g FIBER

2 cups	(500 ml) all-purpose flour
½ cup	(125 ml) all-vegetable shortening
1 tsp	(5 ml) nutmeg
½ cup	(125 ml) granulated sugar
2	egg yolks
¼ cup	(50 ml) softened butter
⅓ cup	(75 ml) light cream
1 cup	(250 ml) icing sugar
2 tbsp	(30 ml) lemon juice

1 tbsp	(15 ml) hot water
	pinch salt
	grated rind 1 orange

Preheat oven to 350°F (180°C).

Place flour, salt, shortening, nutmeg, granulated sugar and orange rind in bowl.

Add egg yolks and butter; incorporate well with pastry blender.

Add cream and pinch dough to incorporate. Roll on floured surface until about ¼ inch (0.65 cm) thick. Dust with more flour if needed.

Using assorted cookie cutters, cut shapes and place on buttered cookie sheet. Bake 12 minutes.

Meanwhile, mix remaining ingredients together for glaze.

As soon as cookies are done, brush tops with lemon glaze.

Cool cookies on wire racks.

Place flour, salt, shortening and nutmeg in bowl.

Add granulated sugar and orange rind.
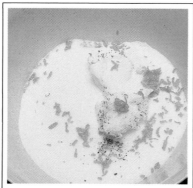

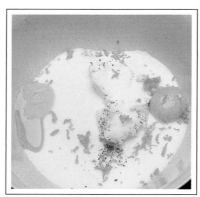
Add egg yolks.

Add butter and incorporate well with pastry blender.

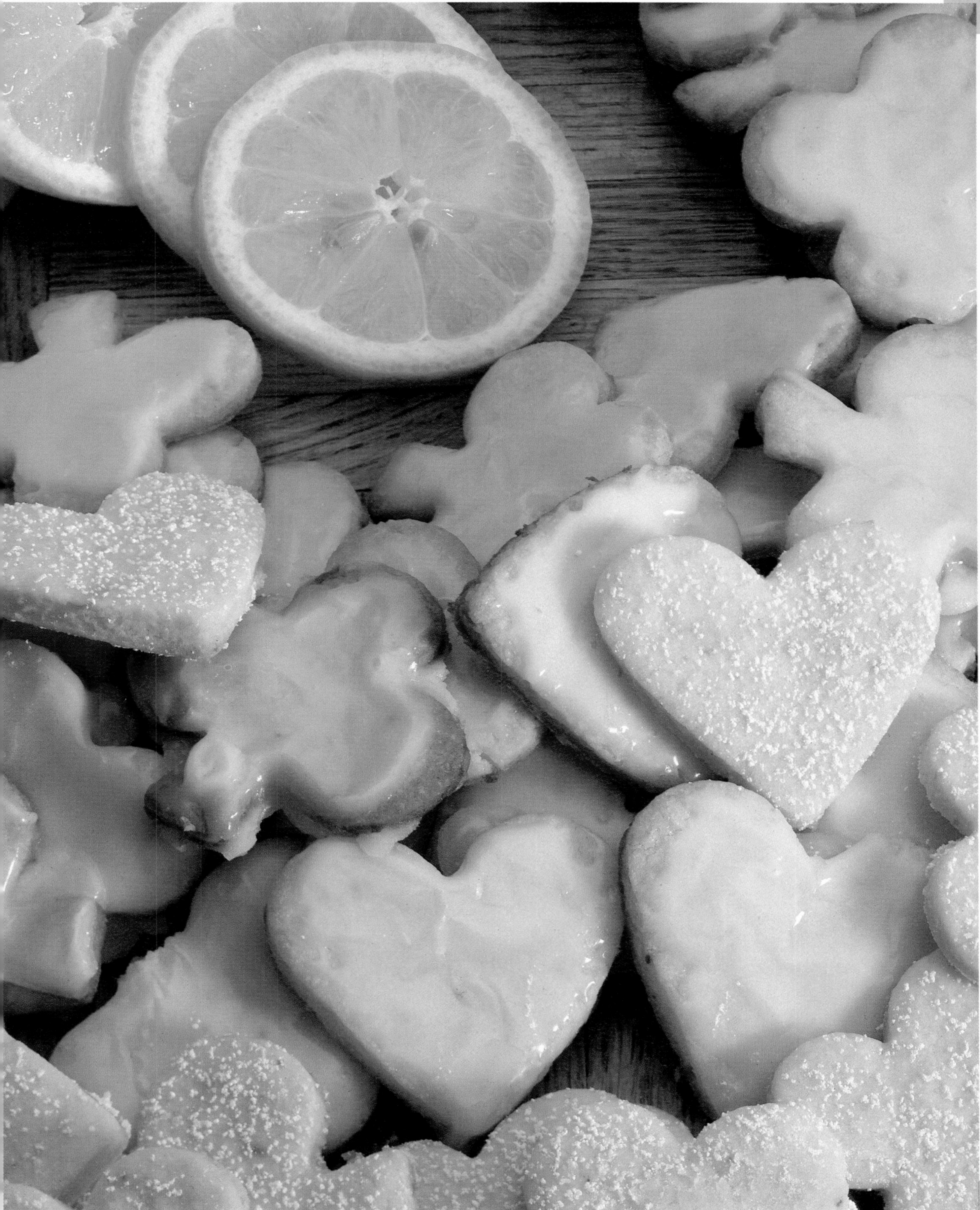

Almond Cookies

(yield: 24-36)

2 COOKIES	152 CALORIES	15g CARBOHYDRATE
3g PROTEIN	9g FAT	0.1g FIBER

¾ cup	(175 ml) softened butter
½ cup	(125 ml) granulated sugar
¾ cup	(175 ml) ground almonds
1¾ cups	(425 ml) all-purpose flour
¼ cup	(50 ml) light cream
2 tbsp	(30 ml) cold water

Place butter, sugar and almonds in bowl; cream together.

Add flour and incorporate with pastry blender.

Pour in cream and pinch dough with fingers.

Add water, incorporate and shape dough into ball. Cover with waxed paper and refrigerate 1 hour.

Preheat oven to 350°F (180°C).

Place dough on floured surface and roll until about ¼ inch (0.65 cm) thick. Dust with more flour if needed.

Using assorted cookie cutters, form shapes and place on buttered cookie sheet. Bake 10-12 minutes.

Cool cookies on wire racks.

Anise Cookies

(yield: 24-36)

2 COOKIES	102 CALORIES	21g CARBOHYDRATE
2g PROTEIN	1g FAT	0.1g FIBER

3	eggs
1 cup	(250 ml) granulated sugar
2 cups	(500 ml) all-purpose flour
1 tsp	(5 ml) baking powder
1 tbsp	(15 ml) anise seeds

Place eggs in large bowl and add sugar; mix together.

In separate bowl, sift flour with baking powder. Drop in anise seeds and mix.

Incorporate flour into wet batter. Cover with waxed paper and refrigerate dough overnight.

Preheat oven to 350°F (180°C).

Place cookie dough on floured surface and roll dough until about ¼ inch (0.65 cm) thick. Sprinkle with additional flour to avoid sticking.

Using cookie cutters (of different shapes if desired), form shapes and place cookies on buttered cookie sheet. Bake 10 minutes.

Cool cookies on wire racks.

Party Cookies

(yield: 24-36)

2 COOKIES	119 CALORIES	13g CARBOHYDRATE
1g PROTEIN	7g FAT	0g FIBER

½ cup	(125 ml) softened butter
¾ cup	(175 ml) granulated sugar
1 oz	(30 g) grated semi-sweet chocolate
1	egg
¼ cup	(50 ml) shredded coconut
1¼ cups	(300 ml) all-purpose flour
1 tsp	(5 ml) baking powder
	pinch salt
	green sprinkles

Place butter, sugar and chocolate in bowl; cream together with electric beater.

Add egg and continue beating.

Mix in coconut. Sift flour with baking powder and salt; incorporate into wet batter. Cover with waxed paper and refrigerate 3 hours. Preheat oven to 350°F (180 °C).

Place cookie dough on floured surface and roll dough until about ¼ inch (0.65 cm) thick. Sprinkle with additional flour to avoid sticking.

Shower dough with green sprinkles and cut into shapes with cookie cutters.

Place cookies on buttered cookie sheet and bake 10 minutes. Cool on wire racks.

Place butter, sugar and chocolate in bowl; cream together with electric beater.

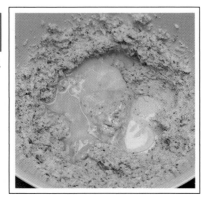

Add egg and continue beating.

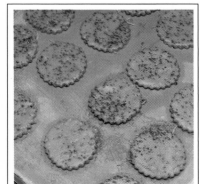

Mix in coconut. Sift flour with baking powder and salt; incorporate into wet batter. Cover with waxed paper and refrigerate 3 hours.

Place prepared cookies on buttered sheet and bake 10 minutes.

Chocolate Tube Cake   *(serves 8-10)*

1 SERVING	424 CALORIES	27g CARBOHYDRATE
10g PROTEIN	31g FAT	0.2g FIBER

8 oz	(250 g) sweet chocolate
½ cup	(125 ml) strong black coffee
2 tbsp	(30 ml) Tia Maria liqueur
10	egg yolks
½ cup	(125 ml) granulated sugar
10	egg whites
1½ cups	(375 ml) heavy cream, whipped with dash vanilla
½ cup	(125 ml) slivered almonds

Preheat oven to 350°F (180°C). Butter 2 cookie sheets and cover each with sheet of buttered waxed paper.

Place chocolate, coffee and liqueur in stainless steel bowl (or double-boiler) and place over saucepan half-filled with boiling water. Allow chocolate to melt, then remove and set aside to cool.

Place egg yolks in bowl and add granulated sugar; beat with electric beater about 3-4 minutes.

Stir in melted chocolate and continue beating 2-3 minutes. Place bowl in refrigerator 5-6 minutes.

Beat egg whites until stiff. Incorporate ⅓ into cooled chocolate mixture, mixing with spatula.

Add remaining egg whites and fold in with spatula, scraping bottom of bowl to incorporate. Turn bowl during this procedure and be careful not to overmix!

Pour batter onto prepared cookie sheets and spread evenly with spatula. Bake 15 minutes.

Turn off oven. With door ajar, let cakes stand 10 minutes.

Remove from oven and let cool 5-6 minutes.

Spread whipped cream over cakes and sprinkle with almonds. Delicately detach cake from waxed paper while rolling it onto itself.

Completely rid of old waxed paper, wrap chocolate tubes in new waxed paper and refrigerate 12 hours before serving.

Place egg yolks in bowl and add granulated sugar; beat with electric beater about 3-4 minutes.

Stir in melted chocolate and continue beating 2-3 minutes.

Incorporate ⅓ of beaten egg whites into cooled chocolate mixture. Mix with spatula.

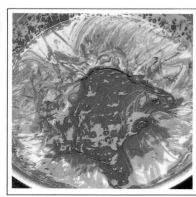

Add remaining egg whites and fold with spatula, scraping bottom of bowl, to incorporate.

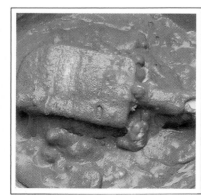

Shortbread Cookies

(yield: 24-36)

2 COOKIES	179 CALORIES	19g CARBOHYDRATE
1g PROTEIN	11g FAT	0.1g FIBER

½ lb	(250 g) softened, unsalted butter
½ cup	(125 ml) icing sugar
½ cup	(125 ml) cornstarch
1½ cups	(375 ml) all-purpose flour
1 tsp	(5 ml) cinnamon
	pinch salt
	candied cherries, halved

Preheat oven to 325°F (160°C).

Place butter in food processor. Add sugar and mix 2-3 minutes.

Add cornstarch, flour, cinnamon and salt; continue mixing until well blended.

Roll dough between the palms of your hands into small balls. Place on buttered and floured cookie sheet and flatten with tines of fork. Top with candied cherries.

Bake 14 minutes. Cool cookies on wire racks.

Place softened, unsalted butter in bowl of food processor.

Add icing sugar.

Mix 2-3 minutes.

Add remaining ingredients, except cherries, and continue mixing until well blended.

Royal Biscuits

(yield: 24-36)

2 COOKIES	155 CALORIES	21g CARBOHYDRATE
2g PROTEIN	7g FAT	0.3g FIBER

1 cup	(250 ml) all-purpose flour
¾ tsp	(3 ml) baking soda
1 tsp	(5 ml) baking powder
½ tsp	(2 ml) ground cloves
1 cup	(250 ml) brown sugar
½ cup	(125 ml) softened butter
1	beaten egg
1 tsp	(5 ml) vanilla
1 cup	(250 ml) quick-cooking rolled oats
½ cup	(125 ml) shredded coconut
	pinch salt

Place flour, baking soda, baking powder, cloves and salt in bowl; stir and set aside.

Cream brown sugar and butter in another bowl using spatula.

Stir in egg and vanilla; mix with electric beater.

Add rolled oats and coconut; incorporate well with spatula.

Fold in flour mixture and mix until completely incorporated. Cover with sheet of waxed paper and refrigerate 2-3 hours.

Preheat oven to 350°F (180°C).

When ready to bake cookies, roll dough on floured surface until about ¼ inch (0.65 cm) thick.

Using assorted cookie cutters, form shapes and place on buttered cookie sheet. Bake 10 minutes.

Cool cookies on wire racks.

These wholesome biscuits are a perfect companion for afternoon breaks.

Cream brown sugar and butter together using spatula.

Stir in egg and vanilla; then mix with electric beater.

Add rolled oats and coconut; incorporate well with spatula.

Fold in flour mixture and mix until completely incorporated.

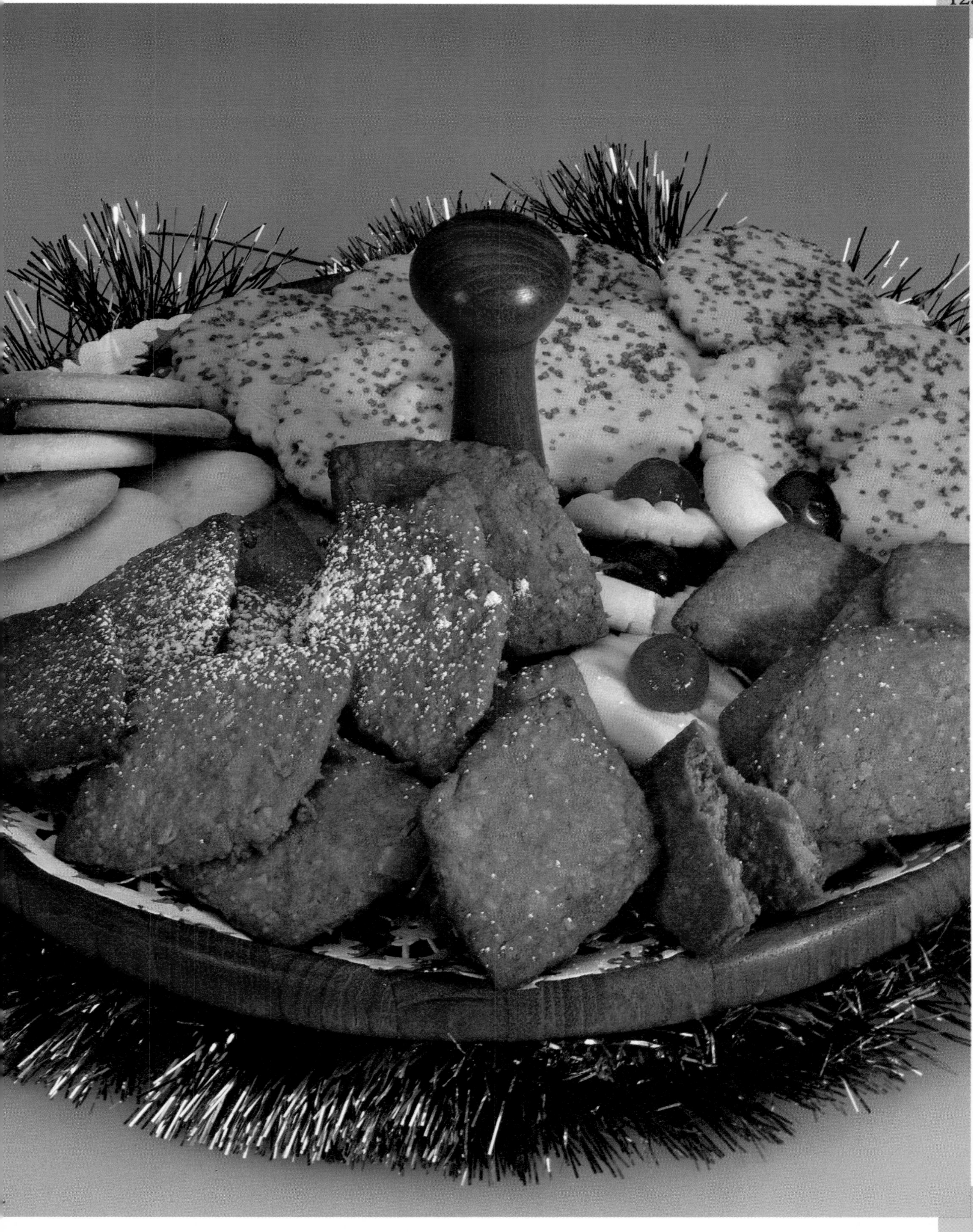

Cheese Parfait

(serves 2-4)

1 SERVING	505 CALORIES	19g CARBOHYDRATE
6g PROTEIN	45g FAT	3.1g FIBER

8 oz	(250 g) package cream cheese, softened
3 tbsp	(45 ml) brown sugar
2 tbsp	(30 ml) Tia Maria liqueur
½ cup	(125 ml) heavy cream, whipped
1 cup	(250 ml) chopped fresh strawberries
	whole fresh strawberries for decoration

Place cheese in bowl of electric mixer. Add sugar and mix well for 2 minutes.

Add Tia Maria and continue mixing 30 seconds.

Add whipped cream and chopped strawberries; incorporate using spatula until well blended.

Spoon mixture into parfait glasses and refrigerate 3-4 hours before serving.

Decorate with fresh strawberries.

Walnut Chocolate Chewies

(serves 6-8)

1 SERVING	298 CALORIES	24g CARBOHYDRATE
6g PROTEIN	20g FAT	1.0g FIBER

1 cup	(250 ml) chopped walnuts
1 cup	(250 ml) slivered almonds
½ cup	(125 ml) liquid honey
2 tbsp	(30 ml) strong black coffee
	sweet cocoa to taste

Place walnuts and almonds in small bowl and toss together. Transfer to food processor and blend several minutes.

Replace nuts in small bowl and add honey; mix together.

Transfer nuts back to food processor and add coffee; blend about 1 minute.

Spread mixture on large plate and cover with sheet waxed paper, pressed against surface. Refrigerate 2-3 hours.

Remove and shape into small balls with hands. Roll in cocoa and continue to chill another hour before serving.

1 Place walnuts and almonds in small bowl and toss together.

2 Replace blended nuts in bowl and add honey; mix together.

3 Transfer nuts back to food processor and add coffee.

4 Blend about 1 minute.

Coffee Custard Pudding

(serves 6)

1 SERVING	174 CALORIES	12g CARBOHYDRATE
5g PROTEIN	12g FAT	0g FIBER

1 cup	(250 ml) hot milk
1 cup	(250 ml) hot, light cream
2 tbsp	(30 ml) hot expresso coffee or very strong coffee
1 tbsp	(15 ml) rum
⅓ cup	(75 ml) granulated sugar
4	eggs
	whipped cream

Preheat oven to 350°F (180°C).

Pour milk, cream and coffee into bowl; whisk together.

Add rum and beat with electric beater.

Add sugar and continue beating to incorporate.

Lightly beat eggs with fork. Pour into bowl containing custard mixture and whisk well until incorporated.

Place 6 individual custard dishes in roasting pan and pour in 1 inch (2.5 cm) hot water.

Fill custard dishes with mixture and bake 40 minutes.

Cool before unmolding and refrigerate. Before serving decorate with whipped cream.

Molasses Custard

(serves 6)

1 SERVING	183 CALORIES	14g CARBOHYDRATE
5g PROTEIN	12g FAT	0g FIBER

1 cup	(250 ml) hot milk
1 cup	(250 ml) hot, light cream
4	eggs
⅓ cup	(75 ml) molasses
½ tsp	(2 ml) vanilla
	pinch salt
	whipped cream

Preheat oven to 350°F (180°C).

Pour milk and cream into bowl; whisk well.

Lightly beat eggs with fork. Add to bowl along with molasses, salt and vanilla; whisk very well.

Place 6 individual custard dishes in roasting pan and pour in 1 inch (2.5 cm) hot water.

Fill custard dishes with mixture and bake 40 minutes.

Cool before unmolding and refrigerate. Before serving decorate with whipped cream.

Eggnog

(serves 4-6)

1 SERVING	257 CALORIES	21g CARBOHYDRATE
8g PROTEIN	12g FAT	0g FIBER

4	eggs, separated
½ cup	(125 ml) fine sugar
¼ cup	(50 ml) rum
2 tbsp	(30 ml) cognac
2 cups	(500 ml) cold milk
1 cup	(250 ml) cold, light cream
2	egg whites
	pinch nutmeg

Beat egg yolks with electric beater. Add half of sugar and continue beating until thick.

Pour in rum and cognac; beat 1 minute.

Add milk and cream; continue beating 30 seconds.

Place all egg whites in bowl. Beat with electric beater until they peak. Add remaining sugar and continue beating 1 minute.

Using spatula, fold in egg whites until well incorporated.

Serve in glasses with dash of nutmeg.